The Power of
the Second Thought

The Power of the Second Thought
How to Live With Indestructible Hope

Jesse Bradley

Published by Game Changer Publishing

Paperback ISBN: 978-1-962656-28-3
Hardcover ISBN: 978-1-962656-29-0
Digital: ISBN: 978-1-962656-30-6

www.GameChangerPublishing.com

DEDICATION

To my wonderful wife, Laurie.
You consistently, unselfishly, and passionately serve our family and
community.
Everything you do is for Jesus, and you are inspiring in the deepest way.
I love you and thank God for all of our adventures together.

Scan this QR code to access free resources on hope! This includes Jesse's "7 Days of Transformation" video series and content related to personal development, inspiration, faith, family, and relationships.

Scan the QR Code Here:

The Power of
the Second Thought

How to Live With Indestructible Hope

Jesse Bradley

www.GameChangerPublishing.com

ACKNOWLEDGMENTS

Thank you to Jeff Johnson, who walked closely with me in the darkest days and mentored me with integrity, insights, and compassion.

Thanks to my family, who have loved me unconditionally and beyond words. You have been incredibly generous at every stage of my life. I appreciate your sense of humor, too.

I am so grateful for our church family and how we learn from each other and abide with Jesus together daily. Our unity and diversity are a glimpse of heaven.

Thanks to Jeff, Michelle, Wayne, Joel, Brenda, and Ty, who have consistently traveled the extra mile with this project to creatively bring hope to more people in a personal way.

Thank you to our entire staff team who lead, live, and love with a humble dedication that glorifies our great God, who continues to transform lives locally and globally.

Thank you to my four children, Joel, Silas, Lili, and Elijah, who are our treasures. Laurie and I love seeing you grow into all God has designed you to be. God has deposited incredible gifts in each of you. May God's grace, truth, and hope flood your hearts, minds, and souls. Laughing with you always brings so much refreshment and joy.

MEANINGFUL WORDS

"Jesse's message and passion stand out. I remember the first time I heard Jesse speak, I was immediately inspired and impacted. His words are both beautifully articulated and brilliant. Jesse is a man who is in alignment with his calling, and the world is a much brighter place because of it. This is your go-to book for finding hope at a time when we need it more than ever."

– Craig Siegel, WSJ Bestselling Author,
Global Speaker, Podcast Host, and Coach.

"Jesse Bradley brings a powerful passion for evangelism and discipleship to everything he touches. If you want to grow in your personal walk with Jesus, he's the kind of guy you want to hang around and listen to."

– Dr. Larry Osborne, Author and Teaching Pastor,
North Coast Church.

"I have had the privilege of seeing Pastor Jesse serving and leading. He has authentic passion and cares for people in his multiethnic church family and the community at large. Jesse embodies the true essence of compassion and faith. He has consistently provided spiritual guidance and support that has touched the lives of people around the world. He is funny and engaging. If you can give away hope, Jesse would go door-to-door until everyone had an abundance."

– Comedian Nazareth,
Laughter for All Ministries.

"Jesse Bradley brings a message that is needed today. What hits me most is that his message is relevant, timely, practical, and authentic. He views the struggles and issues of life in a way that centers us to what is most important."

Mike Romberger, pastor and former President
and CEO of Mount Hermon Christian Camps.

"Jesse is an innovative, powerful, and fresh voice for the gospel. He talks about Jesus in a way that inspires and draws each of us closer to the God we long for."

– Scott Chapman, Senior Pastor, The Chapel.

Table of Contents

INTRODUCTION

I didn't find hope until I lost it. I was raised on the University of Minnesota campus, with our apartment situated in the football stadium's parking lot. Sports surrounded me; they occupied my thoughts, captivated my heart, and echoed in my earliest memories as I heard the crowd's roar during games that took place just steps away. These games were a lifeline during the frigid Midwest winters.

At just two years old, I declared my aspiration to be a professional athlete. Some people possess a deep clarity about their life's purpose from a young age. My dream became a reality. After graduating from Dartmouth College, celebrating two Ivy League titles, and an Elite 8 appearance in the NCAA tournament, I pursued soccer in Africa. Signing a contract as a goalkeeper for the Highlander's Football Club in Bulawayo, Zimbabwe, was a dream come true. Can you relate to working towards a dream for two decades and finally achieving it?

I cherished Zimbabwe and the dear people who became friends there. Their hospitality, generosity, and the deep connections I made were unparalleled. While life was vibrant on and off the field, the environment included AIDS, poverty, drought, and joblessness. Experiencing these issues first-hand, beyond just reading about them, profoundly affected me. It reshaped my perspective. I endeavored to give back, tutoring students and serving the community.

Yet, for every heart-wrenching story, there was a triumph over adversity. Children's songs filled classrooms, and hope echoed in the streets. Their melodies still resonate with me.

During my season in Zimbabwe, I faced a life-altering tragedy. To guard against malaria, I took a prescribed medication. Over time, this accumulated toxic levels in my system. The side effects were debilitating, affecting my heart rate, causing migraines, and bringing on waves of anxiety and depression. The medication was intended to protect me but was, instead, poisoning me.

I returned to the U.S., seeking medical assistance, but no clear answers or recovery were in sight. For a year, I grappled with my health. My capabilities, identity, and mental well-being felt robbed from me. I spiraled into hopelessness.

It took a decade for me to fully heal. My journey to recovery was multifaceted; some aspects were deeply personal and introspective, while others were proactive. Some progress was swift; much was painstakingly slow. A C.S. Lewis quote from *The Problem of Pain* resonated with me: "We can ignore even pleasure. But pain insists on being attended to. God whispers to us in our pleasures, speaks in our conscience, but shouts in our pains: it is His megaphone to rouse a deaf world."

My faith became a gritty, real struggle, not a tidy, clichéd sentiment. Pain transformed into a tool as God began teaching me about genuine hope. I write about hope because I've experienced its absence. I've navigated numerous soul-wrenching nights. Can you relate to a time when everything you thought was going right abruptly diminishes and crumbles? My plans, joy, and trajectory were upended by factors beyond my control. Life would never be the same. The highs of my ascent lasted years, yet the descent brought it crashing down in mere weeks. A sudden, uncontrollable tragedy altered my life's course forever. Has life ever blindsided you?

A New Hope

In my darkest hour, my story didn't end. I am convinced that during our worst moments, God is doing His most profound work. I found hope, both a gift to accept and a habit to cultivate, during my lowest valleys. This time of healing led to shifts in my identity, beliefs, attitude, thinking, relationships, and faith. My suffering carved out a new passion and purpose in me. Valleys, not mountaintops, bear the most fruit.

If you're weathering a storm, having lost someone or something significant, know your story is not over. I don't belittle your pain. Grief can be prolonged, and healing gradual. Yet, there is hope more real and uplifting than your most formidable challenges—a hope both relational and habitual.

In recent years, institutions like the Census Bureau, the CDC, and the American Psychological Association report alarming levels of stress, hopelessness, overdose deaths, and mental health crises. In their quest for answers, people often feel starved for hope. Hope feeds our soul, invigorates our vision, inspires us, drives us daily, shapes our relationships, and infuses us with life. Aren't we all designed to experience and radiate hope?

If you're depleted of hope or long for a more vibrant quality of life, I'd like to guide you through tangible steps to empower and encourage you. Perhaps you feel overwhelmed, externally successful, but internally adrift. Isolation isn't the answer. Together, like embers, our collective hope can blaze like a bonfire. When hope deserted me, I was desperate, lonely, and confused about recovery. Have you sensed that there is a greater hope available for you?

Abide and Respond

A phrase that significantly aided my journey is "abide and respond." Often, hopeful messages sound like self-help with daunting to-dos. While our actions matter, God's help surpasses self-help. A long, arduous list is not what an exhausted soul needs. Hope is like an oasis on a sweltering day. A reservoir filled with God's love, peace, and promises.

"Abide" emphasizes closeness to God and receptiveness. Reside and linger in God's presence, receiving from our compassionate, benevolent, and kind Creator. Abiding encompasses accepting His grace, love, perspective, truth, goodness, and hope. It's about embracing, not striving. God's greatest gift to us is His presence.

The hope you crave isn't predicated or contingent on your achievements. You need to take action and develop habits, but first, you must receive. Prioritize receiving, both in significance and sequence.

If the idea of abundant peace, joy, and hope is new to you, embrace it. Realize that God's love doesn't depend on your accomplishments. This realization requires humility. Hope is primarily a gift to be received.

We're not designed for solitary existence. We need God, community, and hope. It seems simple, but life's cruelties often challenge this sentiment. Despite our best intentions, we often stray. I will share what helped and hindered me.

Together, we journey and learn. I live by these teachings daily. I share them because I would have benefited if someone had imparted them to me at the outset of my hope journey. Will you let me accompany you on this path? Discovering hope entails changes and challenging the status quo. To embrace the rich and overflowing hope that God offers, we must dispel lies, negative habits, limiting beliefs, and obstacles to hope. Are you ready to commence a fresh chapter in your life?

Hope and Healing

Out of the ashes of my life, God's grace has brought a new song of joy. God led me through those years, despite my resistance, to share my story with greater vulnerability than I ever intended. I was in denial for a long time. Many people pulled me out of the darkness. Although I wanted to keep my journey private, God moved me forward. To be honest, I'm a reluctant writer. You never know what will unfold when you say "Yes" to God. What is God communicating to you, and what is He calling you to do? There's a fire burning within me because I understand the immense healing that's available. Hope brings healing.

Over the past three years, I felt God urging me to take risks. I saw the hopelessness during the pandemic and felt called to share my story. I've relayed this message in countless conversations and counseling sessions with individuals suffering from tragedies and trauma. Taking a new step meant connecting with a larger audience. Looking back, God has opened doors to share His message of hope with many, including regular appearances on major television networks and programs like Good Morning America, NBC News, Fox, CBS Sports, and various international media networks. My desire is to simply be where people are and connect in an authentic way. What brings me the deepest joy is witnessing transformed lives. The focus isn't on the number of people or platforms. I share this to encourage you to trust God and be open, available, and committed to sharing His message.

I'm convinced people crave hope more than they can express. The hope God offers is personal, robust, and ultimately unbreakable. I believe that hope shapes our actions. Often, we settle for a limited amount of hope rather than the abundance God offers. Hope is essential, caught, and taught. As we share our stories, our hope grows.

You might be wondering, *Is this worth my investment of time and energy?* I offer a roadmap to show where we'll travel together. The larger picture encompasses three elements of hope: desiring, discovering, and developing. I will present a practical plan, including specific next steps and daily hope cultivation. We'll identify hope thieves and false hopes and eliminate them from our lives. Hope is both relational and habitual. *The Power of the Second Thought* is a transformative tool. By focusing on this concept, the hope in your life will become evident internally, externally, and spiritually.

Moreover, I've created videos to reinforce the book's content. The QR codes at the end of each chapter give you access to these personal messages and prayers. Additionally, each chapter has Bible study questions, allowing a deeper exploration individually or with a group. Together, we'll draw close to the God of hope, letting our lives overflow with it.

You're in the right place if you're seeking growth and more hope in your life. Have you felt the urge to reignite a passion that's been missing? This content will be invaluable if you've felt stuck or know the depths of hopelessness. There are new solutions, perspectives, and powerful, transformative habits. Hope is available, relational, habitual, and indestructible.

Hope shines when an orphan finds a family, an alcoholic tastes freedom, or a wandering soul returns to God. A self-centered individual can start serving their community, and people from different nations begin to unite in love.

My prayer is that God will empower you and transform your inner life with His shalom, joy, and grace, and your foundation will be solid, like a house on the rock, not sand. We need this hope today. Often, we've unintentionally rejected or belittled hope. However, it offers the richest way to live. Your story is not over. Are you ready to experience God's abundant and indestructible hope?

Cultivating Hope:

1. What are some of the reasons you have hope?

2. When have you lost hope?

3. What do you want to gain from this book?

Bible Study Questions:

1. What does it mean that your Creator is the God of hope?

"May the God of hope fill you with all joy and peace as you trust in him, so that you may overflow with hope by the power of the Holy Spirit." (Romans 15:13)

2. How does hope lead to rest and contentment?

"Yes, my soul, find rest in God; my hope comes from him. Truly he is my rock and my salvation; he is my fortress, I will not be shaken." (Psalm 62:5-6)

3. How does God's love change the amount of hope you have?

"The Lord delights in those who fear him, who put their hope in his unfailing love." (Psalm 147:11)

4. In what ways does God renew you and help you to soar?

"But those who hope in the Lord will renew their strength. They will soar on wings like eagles; they will run and not grow weary, they will walk and not be faint." (Isaiah 40:31)

5. Why does God sing over you?

"The Lord your God is with you, the Mighty Warrior who saves. He will take great delight in you; in his love he will no longer rebuke you, but will rejoice over you with singing." (Zephaniah 3:17)

Scan this QR Code to dive deeper with Jesse and watch his video that provides additional stories, insights, and a prayer:

ELEMENT 1: DESIRE

Move Towards Hope

"Where there is no hope in the future,
there is no power in the present."
– John Maxwell

Hope can be lost as well as found. It is the dynamics of our journey—with its highs and lows—that truly shape us. Every story is significant. Stories are powerful. I'm honored that you would listen to mine, and I pray it encourages and empowers you as you process and share your own. We are all designed to give and receive hope. When hope feels distant, pursue it intentionally, persistently, and consistently.

From the heights of professional soccer, my life flipped upside down in just a few weeks. Moving back in with my parents and taking up residence in their basement bonus room, I was stunned and scared. I struggled to understand how I went from peak physical condition to a calendar full of medical appointments. Sitting still, my heart raced over 160 beats a minute due to frequent episodes of tachycardia. Additionally, I developed an atrial flutter, causing my heart to skip beats continuously. The cardiologist discovered a new heart murmur, and pain plagued the left side of my chest day and night. Sleeping was a challenge, and I felt as though my heart would burst from my chest. As the symptoms persisted for months, I couldn't help but wonder: How much longer could this go on?

To monitor potential emergencies, my parents set up a baby monitor. A prescribed anti-malaria medication had compromised the inhibitors in my heart, throwing its regular rhythms and regulations into disarray. The cardiologists were at a loss, hesitant to introduce new medications because of potential unforeseen interactions. I felt trapped in my own failing body—helpless. I was haunted by fatigue, double vision, sweats, chills, and migraines. As an athlete, control—first of my mind as a goalkeeper, then of my body through fitness and training—was paramount. Now, it felt like everything was spiraling out of my grasp.

The psychological toll was immense. It was like being on a horrific drug trip despite my lack of experience with drugs. Disturbing visions plagued not just my nights but also my waking hours. When the lights went out, my mind conjured bizarre images. Emotional turmoil followed: waves of anxiety, first-time panic attacks, and a crippling depression. I yearned for stability and normalcy. Everything familiar felt miles away. I was grappling with the abrupt end of my professional soccer career—a shattered dream—and was left fighting for my very life. Physically, mentally, and emotionally, I was at my breaking point. I hadn't considered a backup plan. Losing everything seemed a cruel fate, especially when there was no encouraging prognosis of recovery. Have you ever felt truly overwhelmed? It often feels like there's a breaking before remaking, a dead end before a path opens, and a death before a resurrection.

Medical professionals had no answers and no assurances of recovery. But beyond the physical and emotional distress, I was spiritually confused and dry. God felt distant. The pain and loss skewed my perception of Him. Bible passages seemed irrelevant to my plight. I felt distance from God, not by choice, but because of the overwhelming grief and pain. I was stripped of my strength, my control, and my solutions. It's in these moments, when we realize we can't save ourselves that we genuinely turn to God and understand our profound need for Him. Have you endured times like this in your life?

I share this with you because life is unpredictable. You might start on one trajectory only to find you've lost more than you ever deemed possible, leaving you grappling with despair. Our physical, mental, emotional, and spiritual facets are interconnected. There are times when hopelessness dominates our narrative. We feel ensnared, unable to glimpse any light at the end of the tunnel, unable to fathom God's intervention in our predicament. I've always leaned towards optimism, but this despair was unparalleled. I share these details openly so you understand: my message of hope isn't hypothetical or abstract. Often, there's a descent before an ascent, and without death, there's no resurrection. God can bring profound experiences from the direst of circumstances. Let's reflect on Psalm 23.

"The Lord is my shepherd, I lack nothing. He makes me lie down in green pastures, he leads me beside quiet waters, he refreshes my soul. He guides me along the right paths for his name's sake. Even though I walk through the darkest valley, I will fear no evil, for you are with me; your rod and your staff, they comfort me. You prepare a table before me in the presence of my enemies. You anoint my head with oil; my cup overflows. Surely your goodness and love will follow me all the days of my life and I will dwell in the house of the Lord forever."

God is with us in the darkest valleys. We don't remain in those depths; we move forward, guided by His unending hope. We walk through the valley; we do not set up camp there. Jesus, our Good Shepherd, knows sorrow intimately. Truth transcends our feelings. Even when God's hand seems invisible, trust His heart. In times of strife, cling to His Word. Jesus remains faithful. Though we may lose hope, the Messiah never wavers. While we sin, our Savior offers forgiveness. While we face death, God grants eternal life. We deeply and daily need hope, and our King always provides. We are meant to stay connected to, and draw from the One who offers living water. What I learned in the valley of the shadow of death I still carry with me today.

Hope Shifts

Moving towards hope necessitates significant shifts in our habits, attitudes, and relationships. At the pit's depths, I realized that my old coping mechanisms were insufficient. My default response to life's challenges had always been to simply try harder. I'd make minor adjustments, increase my effort, and employ a bit more ingenuity. While perseverance is commendable, none of these tactics were addressing my issues. I sometimes denied the gravity of my situation, assuring people I was alright. Discussing it felt overwhelming, and I wasn't ready to face the grim reality. I longed to skip ahead to a triumphant recovery, but that seemed increasingly unattainable.

It took a decade for me to fully recover. Denial was futile as the severity of my condition was glaringly obvious. There was no sports field or classroom where I could divert my focus and excel. No quick fix or strategy to cling to. The bleak prognosis from doctors left me feeling utterly isolated and despondent.

Yet, there's a silver lining: God provides us with comfort, guidance, correction, teaching, encouragement, peace, and training. Although I was in survival mode, God was initiating an intricate process of transformation within me. My arrogance was shattered, making way for humility and a stronger relationship with God. I began to adopt what I now term "hope habits" grounded in scripture. They truly made a difference.

The ordeal made me reassess my life, leading to numerous transformative shifts. My initial desire for hope was minuscule, but even a seed of desire can be magnified by God's touch. My faith deepened as I immersed myself in the scriptures and devoted time to worship and abiding with Jesus. I realized that His ways and thoughts far surpassed my understanding. I'd like to share some pivotal hope shifts.

At life's lowest points, recognizing God's unwavering presence, love, and wisdom is essential. It's crucial to understand that your journey isn't over. Reject complacency, resist the pull towards passivity, and combat the deceit of despair. Here are some steps that rekindled my hope:

Listening to God

One fundamental shift was attuning myself to God's voice. Our world is awash with distractions, but Jesus taught that His followers would recognize and cherish His voice. Tuning into God's voice was life-saving for me. Here's why:

God communicates through His Spirit and Word. When I returned to America, the prescribed malaria prevention medication, which had accumulated to toxic levels in my system, was recommended for continued use to ward off potential latent malaria. Medical experts, unaware of my deteriorating condition's cause, were adamant about maintaining the drug regimen, fearing the potential risk of contracting malaria.

It wasn't until a Stanford physician identified the medication's side effects as a possible culprit. This revelation prompted me to pray intensely. During this time, I distinctly felt God's gentle whisper, pointing to the medication as the root cause. While I respect medical professionals and value their expertise, in this instance, they were tragically mistaken. Following God's revelation and my instinct, I made the bold decision to discontinue the medication, in spite of the exhortation from all of my physicians to continue taking the prescribed drug.

To further confirm my conviction, blood samples were sent to the Center for Disease Control. The results revealed toxic levels of the medication in my system. I had been following the prescription for months. Had I not heeded God's guidance and continued the treatment, I'm uncertain if I'd still be here today. God's ability to intervene, to guide through the most harrowing circumstances with unwavering love and truth, is unparalleled. My hope was revitalized by drawing closer to Him, valuing, and trusting His guidance. Listen to His whispers. God communicates with you, and God is faithful.

Vulnerable Prayers

Here's a revelation from my second hope shift. Before encountering this tragedy and trauma, my prayers were concise, more intellectual, and theological. However, I found solace in Psalm 62:8:

> *"Trust in him at all times, you people; pour out your hearts to him, for God is our refuge."*

This was transformative for me. I would ponder on its urging to pour out one's heart to God and trust Him always, yet I struggled with how to genuinely do that. How could I cultivate such a habit, especially as a new Christian? I discovered it entails sharing with God both your circumstances and emotions. Tell God about your feelings and thoughts. God, being all-knowing, won't be caught off guard by your confessions. Yet, such openness fortifies trust and deepens your connection. Moreover, it reshapes you as you honestly and vulnerably communicate with Him.

As I began to open up to God and entrust Him with my burdens, I felt Him take on those weights, which were too overbearing for me alone. The relief and liberation were profound. I had presumed that God might be disinclined to engage with all this, but the reality is that He earnestly desires to bear our burdens. His care emanates from His profound compassion. In surrendering my burdens to Him, I acknowledge my dependence on Him, and such reliance is spiritually healthy and nourishing. As I leaned into Him in new ways to alleviate the stress and burdens I couldn't bear on my own, our bond grew stronger. It is powerful when you realize you are completely known and loved.

A Change in Perspective

The third hope shift precipitated a significant change in my perception and expectations. My prior view of God was that He only took an interest in me when I was flourishing - acquiring an Ivy League degree, excelling as a goalkeeper, treating others well, or meeting needs. I operated under the assumption that God's affection for me surged with every success and accomplishment. Little did I realize that God was equally, if not more, invested in the tumultuous and messy segments of my life.

God cared deeply about my battles with sin, the moments I grappled with temptations, the moments of discouragement and despair, and the instances where I felt adrift, uncertain about my future. I faced insecurity, loneliness, and immense anxiety. Who would want to accompany someone in such turmoil? The answer is Jesus. As I recognized and embraced God's desire to engage with these facets of my life, I concurrently started letting others in, taking relational risks. While I wasn't accustomed to displaying emotion, particularly in tears, I began allowing certain individuals to witness that vulnerability. This was a monumental shift for me, signaling the avenues through which God was instilling healing and hope.

One primary vessel through which God infuses hope is the fostering of genuine, deep, and loving relationships. Authentic connections flourish when there's mutual trust and support, where each person feels unguarded and understood. This new vulnerability with God mirrored my interactions with those who cared about me. As this unfolded, my reservoir of hope expanded. Although God's love often manifests through others, healing doesn't commence until we expose our wounds. Revealing usually precedes healing.

Finding Community

The fourth hope shift revolved around forging new relationships and building a fresh community. Moving from Minnesota to California was a reset. On returning from Africa and relocating to my parents' basement, establishing new connections was imperative. It's one thing to make friends when everything seems perfect, but how do you do so from a place of desolation? The journey was not without its challenges.

Friendships involve considerable risk and discernment. The company we keep profoundly impacts our lives, hinting at our future trajectories. Building community is an intentional decision that includes taking action. Extricating myself from isolation was crucial, as hope blossomed with connection. I sought out individuals whose lives displayed both truth and love. Many new friendships were anchored in Jesus. Their love for God gave me hope that they'd extend the same to me. Those memories forged during the roughest patches of life remain indelible. While some might be tempted to resort to isolation after experiencing betrayal, true happiness can't be found only in solitude. The right community paves the way for restoration and renewed hope. For example, I had many friends like Jeff Johnson, who I could call anytime, discuss any topic, and share my heart freely. Being able to share my feelings and cry with someone like Jeff, who would grieve with me and pray for me, brought so much healing. Real community is a gift from God.

Choosing Gratitude

Another paradigm shift for me was the cultivation of gratitude. I term it 'gritty gratitude' as it involves being thankful even when it's challenging. Although I had a litany of reasons to be discouraged, I chose to focus on my blessings, inspired by the people of Zimbabwe and biblical teachings. Establishing a daily routine of listing ten things I was thankful for and acknowledging them to God was transformative.

What are the benefits of thanking God, and what does gratitude to God create?

1. Stress reduction.

2. Avoiding fixation on what's lacking.
3. Fostering closer relationships.
4. Honoring God.
5. Overcoming setbacks.
6. Breaking out of stagnation.
7. Reviving the spirit and creativity.
8. Enhancing physical well-being.
9. Opening doors to new opportunities.
10. Strengthening resolve.

I was so overwhelmed by how much I lost that I became consumed by the loss, forgetting what I actually still had. By writing down 10 things every day, I connected with God and was able to remain thankful. "I thank you, God, for my clothes, for a hot shower today, and for a comfortable bed. I thank you, God, for my parents. I thank you for the blueberry muffins from Costco today." I would make a list of 10 specific things and then recite them out loud to God every day. I wanted more than just general gratitude; gratitude is not merely a concept. It's an integral part of a relationship. Thankfulness, desire, and hope are all relational. I would express these sentiments out loud to God, verbalizing them with details. Gratitude is indeed powerful, and God is worthy of our thankfulness.

Spiritual Nourishment

Another pivotal shift in hope was when I delved into reading the Bible. I began with three chapters daily and gradually expanded. I highlighted verses and took notes, reflecting on God's promises and His character. This immersion into the Scriptures was nourishing in the deepest ways, and I actively applied what I learned to my life. I started memorizing verses, jotting them down on blank 8.5 x 11 sheets—verses that inspired, healed, and transformed me. Filling my mind, soul, and heart with God's word was a practice I hadn't adopted before.

Growing up, I hadn't engaged with the Bible. I didn't believe God even existed. Since my twenties, however, I've read through it every year. To me, there's no habit more meaningful than spending time with God and immersing oneself in the Scriptures. Some structure, along with an open heart, makes room in our lives for the Holy Spirit to uncover new layers and truths within God's Word. One helpful acronym is SOAP:

- **Scripture**: Read a passage.
- **Observe**: Understand its context and content.
- **Apply**: Interpret its teachings and integrate them into your life.
- **Pray**: Seek God's presence and guidance in your faith journey.

Celebrate Restoration

Another hope shift was recognizing and celebrating my progress. There was a period when even a casual walk would dangerously elevate my heart rate. Using a heart monitor, I observed its sudden escalation even on flat terrains. It was discouraging and deflating when small inclines became challenges. Monitoring my pulse regularly was essential for my health. Though my energy was limited, I began charting my walking progress. It was essential to visualize any advancements, no matter how slight, especially during a prolonged recovery where progress often seemed stagnant. With each improvement, hope grew. This visible progress was a beacon amidst the numerous setbacks in my life. The chart covered my bedroom wall.

God renews us daily, bringing healing on various fronts. I celebrated this recovery and also focused on healthier eating, treasuring the gift of health. Every factor, every bit of energy counted. I now aim to maximize my service to God and others, recognizing the importance of good habits, like ample sleep and nutritious food. Our bodies are temples belonging to God, and it's our role to steward what God provides. When you nearly lose your life, you don't take your health for granted.

New Purpose

I felt God bringing a new direction that was gradually emerging in my life. From being a professional soccer player, I transitioned over many years to becoming a pastor. It began modestly with volunteering at church and tutoring students. Discovering my capacities post-illness was difficult. Despite some setbacks during my volunteer stints, I persisted. Service brings life. Jesus serves, and we're designed to do the same. Serving not only blesses others but enriches us and glorifies God.

While my faith journey was still young, I sometimes felt directionless. However, it's vital to keep moving, even if it's just one step at a time. It is hard to steer a parked car. My continued faith steps led me to school for a graduate degree in theology. A former atheist, I sensed God's calling into ministry. Every step included exercising faith, as God provided confirmation and guidance. When God is in it, don't resist it.

A Secure Identity

Another transformative realization was understanding my identity. After experiencing numerous losses, my prior performance-based identity crumbled. This identity, which linked my self-worth to achievements, was an unstable foundation. With the absence of those achievements, I grappled with self-worth.

A performance-based identity is a cruel roller coaster ride of pride and shame, feeling inflated and deflated. It leaves us empty on the inside, with no real security or stability.

But a vital shift occurred. I transitioned from a performance-based identity to a grace-based one. My true identity emerged as a child of God. Freed from the pressures of external validations, I was grounded in a love and identity that was immutable and eternal.

One profound moment exemplifies this journey of hope. During a particularly challenging night when I felt distant from God, an unexpected call from my uncle, a former addict and professional comedian, altered my perspective. He had picked up a Bible, read the Gospel of Mark, and declared his newfound faith, proclaiming, "Jesus is King. Elvis is not King. Jesus is King." Such moments underscore that hope is always available and relational, and God doesn't give up on us or break His promises.

I made numerous "hope shifts" in my life, each one strategically moving me closer to God and cultivating new habits. With every change, my thirst for hope intensified, teaching me how to align with divine purpose. I pray my journey ignites a desire within you for the boundless hope God offers. Which shifts towards hope have you undertaken? May your longing for hope draw you closer to God and His presence, for therein lies the truest form of hope. God's most precious gift to us is His consistent love and presence. If you feel distant from God, there's a portion of scripture that has inspired and redirected me.

"I remain confident of this: I will see the goodness of the Lord in the land of the living. Wait for the Lord; be strong and take heart and wait for the Lord." Psalm 27:13-14

If you've faced hopelessness, profound disappointments, or loss, know that God will accompany you through the depths. Our ascent is guided by Him, the embodiment of all hope. Placing your trust in God paves the way for hope. His wisdom, impeccable timing, and solace persist, even when we find ourselves uneasy amidst change. Let your desire outweigh the challenges of transformation. The rewards, both immediate and eternal, are profound. In this book, I'll share insights on how God will enable you to walk on the heights in an authentic way. Let's continue on this journey together with a hunger for new hope.

Cultivating Hope:

1. How do you usually respond to your biggest challenges in life?

2. What key shifts have you made in your life as you have gained wisdom?

3. How are you intentional with gratitude during the week?

Bible Study Questions:

1. How does Jesus give us a solid foundation?

"Therefore everyone who hears these words of mine and puts them into practice is like a wise man who built his house on the rock. The rain came down, the streams rose, and the winds blew and beat against that house; yet it did not fall, because it had its foundation on the rock. But everyone who hears these words of mine and does not put them into practice is like a foolish man who built his house on sand. The rain came down, the streams rose, and the winds blew and beat against that house, and it fell with a great crash." (Matthew 7:24-27)

2. Why does Jesus want to come into our lives?

"Here I am! I stand at the door and knock. If anyone hears my voice and opens the door, I will come in and eat with that person, and they with me." (Revelation 3:20)

3. How does God's kindness transform us?

"Yet this I call to mind and therefore I have hope: Because of the Lord's great love we are not consumed, for his compassions never fail. They are new every morning; great is your faithfulness." (Lamentations 3:21-23)

4. What is God's will for you today?

"Make sure that nobody pays back wrong for wrong, but always strive to do what is good for each other and for everyone else. Rejoice always, pray continually, give thanks in all circumstances; for this is God's will for you in Christ Jesus. Do not quench the Spirit." (1 Thessalonians 5:16-19)

5. In what ways does God reassure us when He leads us into something new?

"Be strong and courageous. Do not be afraid or terrified because of them, for the Lord your God goes with you; he will never leave you nor forsake you." (Deuteronomy 31:6)

Scan this QR Code to dive deeper with Jesse and watch his video that provides additional stories, insights, and a prayer:

Make Room For Hope

As your desire for hope intensifies, you'll find yourself facing pivotal decisions. Fundamentally, an augmented sense of hope is tethered to creating space in your life for God. For those who appreciate metaphors, this chapter will resonate. Metaphors offer clarity by providing an alternative viewpoint. They can instigate a paradigm shift, helping you evaluate and discern what might be harmful or obstructive in your life, recognizing barriers and limitations. Metaphors provide insights and a thorough exploration of your potential. God wants to help you overcome obstructions and shatter misconceptions, myths, and falsehoods.

I realize metaphors can be abstract and open the door to a wide range of interpretations, but these are the metaphors that have helped me the most. I'll be specific: when you discern what's extraneous and eliminate it, you pave the way for renewed hope and for God to manifest in unprecedented ways. Although God is omnipresent, He chooses to inhabit certain places in unique ways. His desire is to indwell us as we immerse ourselves in Him fully. Trusting and embracing God culminate our development and growth.

Revelation 3:20 states:

"Here I am! I stand at the door and knock. If anyone hears my voice and opens the door, I will come in and eat with that person, and they with me."

Heed His call, welcome Him, and let Jesus guide and love you more profoundly than anyone else. His guidance will far surpass your own self-guidance. Hope knows who to trust.

A New Song

The first metaphor is "A New Song." Throughout the Bible, we encounter mentions of new songs that God introduces. Moreover, there will be new songs in heaven. These new songs symbolize the novel works of God, fresh blessings, rewarding aspects of life we're embracing, and the innovative teachings of God. They denote rejuvenated visions and triumphs, echoing joy and hope. However, if we remain tethered to the old songs, the melodies of the new ones remain unsung.

All of us have archives of old memories, captured much like songs—old tapes that we collect. They can be positive or negative experiences, like songs. Some songs have videos that replay in our minds. It's important not to keep rewinding and replaying the old tapes when they hinder your progress moving forward. We can be grateful for the past and learn from the past, but we should not try to live in the past.

Two specific old songs often replay in our minds, which we must cautiously navigate. The first is "Glory Days." It's indeed splendid to cherish great memories, monumental moments, and life's highlights in retrospect. But, it's equally crucial to recognize that time marches forward. Obsessing over past achievements can lead to stagnancy, causing us to overlook fresh opportunities. I recall my esteemed soccer coach, Christian Akale, often admonishing our team with the words: "No Complacency!" Have you ever met someone who entertains you with tales from their high school years, painting those times as their pinnacle moments, almost as if they long to return? Such conversations might give the impression that they are trapped in that past.

While it's vital to honor such "glory days," it's imperative not to become ensnared by them. Some individuals speak about God's blessings as if His grace has reached its limit in their lives. Contrarily, the most beautiful moments are still on the horizon. With our final abode being heaven, every day on earth is infused with a divine purpose.

The other familiar old tune, "The Dirge," is often colored with blame, shame, regret, and despondency. This melody emerges when we dwell on life's valleys. Anchoring ourselves in past missteps, engaging in blame games, donning the cloak of undue guilt, and incessantly replaying those moments stymies our growth. It's like being imprisoned in a dim, grim dungeon of desolation. But that's not God's vision for us. Jesus is the liberator who sets captives free. New songs symbolize freedom and are brimming with hope. It's time to embrace a fresh melody.

It would have been easy for me to overfocus on my life, the glory days song, before the tragedy in Africa. Another temptation was to lament without hope, the dirge of despair. I had to refuse to be stuck in those seasons of my life. God wanted to do a new work with new lyrics, instruments, and harmony.

Return from Exile

A story in the Bible resonates with me, illustrating both songs—"Glory Days" and "The Dirge." While God intended to lead the people towards a new song, they were hesitant. Solomon, a king with a vision to construct a temple for God, exhibited remarkable generosity. By employing the finest resources, supplies, and craftsmen, he ensured the temple was magnificent. This temple not only glorified God but also drew visitors from across the globe. Temples held significance in Israel's history, yet they posed a risk of becoming idols, leading to a hollow form of religion. Some believed God's influence was confined solely to the temple vicinity.

In modern times, a similar perspective emerges when people regard churches as exclusive sanctuaries where God resides. A bond with God surpasses the confines of a specific day, hour, or location. Don't try to compartmentalize God to Sunday mornings. Numerous individuals today place undue emphasis on the physical place of worship, overlooking the true essence of His presence. While America and Europe boast of grand church structures, many places witness a palpable dearth of dynamic faith. A building, no matter how grand, is secondary. At its best, it is an inspiring edifice with artwork that reinforces and rejuvenates one's faith. Despite possessing a magnificent temple, the Israelites' spiritual connection with God waned. Their defiance culminated in the Babylonian invasion and the subsequent destruction of the temple, marking the end of an illustrious era.

Decades of exile ensued, accompanied by the melancholic notes of "The Dirge." Marked by isolation, mistreatment, and misunderstandings, their existence became arduous. This phase underscored the necessity for spiritual reconnection with God. The pervasive feelings of isolation and despondence during the pandemic echoed these sentiments, with many experiencing a sense of exile and spiritual detachment. Yet, God persistently and personally beckons us to return when we stray.

God's relentless grace surpasses our transgressions. Eventually, the Israelites, aided by God's intervention, were emancipated from their exile and began their journey back home. Leaders like Zerubbabel, Haggai, and Nehemiah shepherded the masses through the spiritual, emotional, and physical facets of the rebuilding phase. This marked God's renewed endeavor at restoration. However, during this time, contrasting melodies arose. Some pined for the past, singing praises of the previous temple's grandeur and yearning for the glorious days Solomon's temple represented. Conversely, others remained ensnared by the song of exile, focusing on the adversities they faced during the Babylonian reign. They resisted the allure of a new song, choosing instead to dwell on the harrowing memories of the past.

Faith Over Fear

God conveyed to His people that there was another option: a new song. How frequently do we present God with just two choices—"Glory Days" and "The Dirge"? God cannot be confined to a structure; the earth itself is His footstool. Similarly, God doesn't fit within restricted paradigms that negate His emerging work, plan, or song. In the Book of Haggai, as the new temple rose, celebrations and tears ensued in tandem. Those who wept were ensnared by comparisons with Solomon's temple. Such comparisons can be deceptive, breeding envy, jealousy, and desolation. When set against the grandeur of the previous temple, the new edifice seemed underwhelming to many. Yet, in Haggai 2:3-5, God reassures and rallies the people to be steadfast.

> *"'Who of you is left who saw this house in its former glory? How does it look to you now? Does it not seem to you like nothing? 'But now be strong, Zerubbabel,' declares the Lord. 'Be strong, Joshua Son of Jozadak, the high priest. Be strong, all you people of the land,' declares the Lord, 'and work. For I am with you,' declares the Lord Almighty. 'This is what I covenanted with you when you came out of Egypt. And my Spirit remains among you. Do not fear.'" (Haggai 2:3-5)*

Amidst the crowd, some hearts remained attuned to God's voice. A faithful remnant always exists, eager for God's fresh melodies, radiating His joy and hope. God nourishes our souls, fostering relationships that usher in a renewed song. His indomitable presence is His ultimate offering, inhabiting our very essence. The church isn't just a building; it's the collective community and spirit of its believers. Each individual is a vessel, a temple for God's Spirit. And while we don't become deities ourselves, we harbor God's presence in our mortal forms and frames. Through Haggai, God foretells that the splendor of this new temple would eclipse that of Solomon's: the glory of the present would surpass that of the past. God whispers to you that the later glory is the greater glory because the best is yet to come.

29

Such a proclamation bewildered many, as the visible attributes of the new temple seemed less imposing. How could this newer structure possess a grander glory? Their faith wavered as they grappled with God's vision, reluctant to embrace His fresh song. Their oversight was not recognizing that the core of their faith resides in God's presence. The Messiah, Jesus, both fully divine and human, was destined to walk this earth and inhabit the new temple, something that didn't transpire in Solomon's era.

We must guard against becoming excessively engrossed in superficial aspects and remain anchored to God's enduring work through changing seasons. Occasionally, our yardsticks of success are more temporal than eternal. While Solomon's era was a blessed era, it wasn't the pinnacle of the narrative. We shouldn't revere monuments, memories, or specific seasons over the Creator.

The painful phase of rebellion and exile cannot be forgotten. Lives were lost, hope waned, and grief was palpable. It's natural to memorialize such periods with songs of sorrow, acknowledging the human experience. However, perpetually dwelling on past sorrows is debilitating and counterproductive. We should commemorate God's restorative powers and embrace the hope and solace He brings. It's time to resonate with the newer harmonies God bestows. But, unfortunately, many remained anchored to past tunes, either of The Glory Days or of The Dirge of Despair. Will you get rid of the old tapes of shame and guilt and make room for God's new playlist? God is not only with you; He also goes ahead of you.

New Vision

When I arrived in the Pacific Northwest, I felt God's guidance leading me to serve as the pastor at Grace Community Church in Auburn. Joining this remarkable church family filled me with gratitude. The church's genesis traces back to the 1950s when Billy Graham delivered the gospel message at

Memorial Stadium in Seattle beneath the towering silhouette of the Space Needle. As he extended an invitation to follow Jesus, a multitude responded, choosing to begin a new relationship with God. These new disciples gathered, giving birth to a church plant with a new song. Over seven decades, Grace Community Church has navigated through its storied journey, witnessing both golden eras and trying phases.

As I began my tenure, I frequently encountered the two prevailing narratives we've talked about. The first, the "glory days," harkened back to a time roughly two decades prior. In those days, the church was in a phase of exponential growth, adding services and broadening its campus. Recollections of packed parking lots and tales of shuttle buses painted a picture of a time when managing the growing congregation was a delightful challenge. These stories, rich in detail, often illuminated the dynamic vitality of that period. Yet, there was an undeniable undertone of comparison with the season that followed, emphasizing the stark contrast and the subsequent wane in vibrancy.

As one might expect, the alternate narrative was a somber "Dirge," recounting the numerous trials the church had weathered. I deeply respect the unwavering commitment of many stalwarts who, despite adversities, persisted in their mission to love, serve, and embody God's hope. While these challenging times undoubtedly tested people's faith, there were mentions of notable moments of joy and accomplishment. Nevertheless, the prevailing sentiment was one of substantial trials. I distinctly recall a conversation with a long-standing member who harbored genuine concerns about Grace's future survival and the need to seek God for restoration and revitalization

Our leadership team embraced the truth in Isaiah 43:19:

"See, I am doing a new thing! Now it springs up; do you not perceive it? I am making a way in the wilderness and streams in the wasteland."

We felt like God was speaking to our hearts and minds, sensing that God was shaping a compelling vision and guiding us toward a fresh season and a new anthem. True hope often encompasses tangible plans and collective steps forward. For instance, as part of our renewed song of hope, we made a deliberate and sacrificial decision to address our debt. We named this endeavor "Taking Down Goliath." Facing a daunting debt of $2.3 million, our church family responded with immense generosity. Gratefully, through God's provision, we now stand debt-free.

At that juncture, our church comprised many seasoned, wise seniors. Their years of unwavering dedication and service to God remain a consistent source of inspiration. While deeply respecting and celebrating our historical roots, we also understand that the steadfastness of past generations sets the stage for the future. The oldest generation mentors the youth, and in return, the contagious energy and passion of the students invigorate the seniors. This is the beauty of a truly multigenerational church. Recognizing a need for nurturing the younger and middle generations, our eldest members gracefully made room, unanchored by some preferred traditions. Today, we rejoice in the harmony and unity experienced across all age groups.

Previously, our congregation was predominantly white. Today, we celebrate a diverse tapestry of ethnicities, cultures, and nationalities. Mirroring our surrounding community, our journey towards new friendships has been meaningful. This mosaic of a wide range of backgrounds not only represents unity but also beautifully reflects the diversity inherent in God's family. As we gather together as one, it is a glimpse of a heavenly gathering comprising every nation and tribe.

Feeling the strains of isolation, we formed life groups that fostered prayer, Bible study, service, and deep friendships. These groups were especially crucial during the pandemic, becoming the heart and soul of our church. Our identity shifted from being a church that had life groups to a church of life groups. These small groups are at the core of who we are as a diverse family. Complementing this, we became proactive, reaching out beyond the confines of our church to connect with the broader community in innovative ways.

While we continued to champion our established ministries, like the prison outreach, we felt the need to diversify our avenues of service. Initiatives like "Drive Thru Prayer" every Friday night were born, where community members could drive in, connect, and share their prayer needs. Collaborating with other churches and partnering with organizations assisting victims of human trafficking, we've witnessed profound transformations. We intentionally united with dozens of churches across the greater Seattle area to strengthen unity and serve together with many initiatives. Our digital outreach expanded to connect with audiences both locally and globally, bringing messages of hope. This digital ministry, with a dedicated media team, has seen hundreds of thousands of people decide to start a relationship with God. All glory belongs to God.

Psalm 115:1 says:

"Not to us, Lord, not to us but to your name be the glory, because of your love and faithfulness."

While these are just glimpses of our renewed vision and song, I'm filled with anticipation for the many ways God will move in the future.

Jesus is the head of the church, and it belongs to Him. Our role lies in staying connected, attuning ourselves to new divine melodies, and yielding to the Holy Spirit's transformative power. Fresh anthems will continue to arise until we enter heaven, where even more divine songs await. Let us never remain tethered to past triumphs or trials. For God continually charts the path ahead.

"Be strong and courageous. Do not be afraid or terrified because of them, for the Lord your God goes with you; he will never leave you nor forsake you. Then Moses summoned Joshua and said to him in the presence of all Israel, "Be strong and courageous, for you must go with this people into the land that the Lord swore to their ancestors to give them, and you must divide it among them as their inheritance. The Lord himself goes before you and will be with you; he will never leave you nor forsake you. Do not be afraid; do not be discouraged." (Deuteronomy 31:6-8)

You can trust God with the future and every new direction He brings. Take a moment now to pause and ask God to direct your steps and lead you with a new song in your heart.

Choosing Your Song

Every day, each one of us makes a choice about the song we sing. Nobody can compel you to embrace a new song. Nobody can push you to welcome more of God's presence into your life. No one can demand that you create space for renewed hope. It's often said that we experience as much of God's presence as we truly desire. The depth of your relationship with God mirrors your inner longing. The song you choose holds profound significance.

I'm not implying that we all possess innate musical talents. Personally, when I sing, my notes often miss the mark. My sense of pitch leaves much to be desired, leading my children to request that I tone it down. My primary singing venues are my car and the shower. Once, while participating in a choir, a fellow member remarked that my singing was a distraction. His statement was true. My piano teacher literally told me I was wasting her time. Trying to learn the saxophone felt impossible. Some people just don't have many musical gifts.

Yet, God has crafted each of us with the capacity to harbor a song. While a song can be taken literally, it often symbolically encapsulates our thoughts,

34

attitudes, faith, and convictions. Transitioning from the nostalgia of the glory days or the melancholy of the dirge to a novel song can be challenging. Numerous individuals and institutions resist this fresh melody, gradually becoming hollowed from within. Renewal neither comes easily nor instantaneously. Embarking on a new song can push our boundaries and test our limits. The cost can be very high, and your commitment must overcome all the criticism. Throughout the Psalms and other scriptural passages, God urges His people to embrace a fresh song, heralding new endeavors and aspirations. When He introduces a new anthem, are we prepared to wholeheartedly accept, vocalize, and dance to its rhythm?

If your repertoire has been dominated by the songs of past glories or the lamentations of the dirge, pivoting to a fresh tune might initially evoke a sense of loss. Instinctively, we often yearn to cling to past success. A part of us remains fiercely protective of our past. There are many meaningful traditions that should continue. Many sacraments, like marriage, are for all generations.

Grief is an inherent aspect of our journey, for transformation often brings pain. Yet, grieving can foster spiritual growth. It's a vital emotional process. Amidst our grief, it's pivotal to acknowledge God's unwavering presence. Our sorrow is tempered by hope, a hope that towers above our despair. Unlike those who grieve in hopelessness, our grief is illuminated by the hope God instills in us. Nonetheless, during periods of mourning, it's not uncommon to momentarily lose sight of this hope, becoming engulfed by the sheer magnitude of loss and change.

If you hold onto a dirge of despair and carry it forward, it can impede the fresh melody God intends to introduce. In our spiritual journey, we must remain receptive, allowing God to manifest the new rhythms He desires to instill within us. Throughout your life, there will be numerous instances where God aids you in transitioning from the nostalgic echoes of the past or the lamentations of a dirge to a renewed tune. The temptation to cling to the past might be powerful, making you feel as if you possess sole custody over your history and destiny. During such times, it's crucial to relinquish control, surrendering all to God's orchestration. Place your trust in the maestro of the melody. Feelings of apprehension or a sense that change is occurring prematurely might arise. In Numbers Chapter 9, the Israelites learned the importance of synchronizing their movements with the cloud, which was a tangible symbol of God's guiding presence. When the cloud lingered, they remained stationary; when it moved, they followed. While some may have preferred their own timelines, God's pacing proved most trustworthy. If I hadn't moved forward with God after my tragic illness, I would not have discovered the hope He wanted to provide. It takes faith and courage to keep taking the next step. It's worth it!

While traditions are both cherished and vital, we must remember their core significance. Baptisms will perpetually be held, and communion will be observed until we unite with Jesus in eternity. These sacraments beautifully interlink our past, present, and future. For instance, communion hearkens back to Christ's sacrifice on the cross while emphasizing our contemporary unity as believers and foreshadowing Christ's eventual return and the grand celebration that follows. Baptism, similarly, recalls Jesus' crucifixion and resurrection, signifying our rebirth in Him and propelling our gaze towards the promised new heaven and earth where eternal joy awaits. It's paramount to uphold and celebrate these traditions.

However, our spiritual trajectory isn't regressive; we're beckoned forward with God. Our very anatomy—our eyes, arms, legs, feet—propels us onward. While we must honor and glean wisdom from our past, becoming ensnared by it is detrimental. Neither the highs of yesteryears nor the valleys of distress should be deified.

"Hope is the thing with feathers
That perches in the soul
And sings the tune without words
And never stops at all." - Emily Dickinson

Echoing Jesus' teachings, it's imprudent to pour new wine into old wineskins. When God orchestrates a novel tune, it's imperative that we introspect, ensuring no deep-rooted idols or legalistic traditions obstruct or dampen the upcoming symphony. As carriers of hope, we must anticipate God's evolving compositions. Create space in your life for heaven's harmony, the cadence of an intimate journey with God, and the divine tunes intended for every facet of your existence. Rest assured, the most exhilarating chapters are on the horizon. I wanted to emphasize this point because many people never really move beyond the past, and their hope remains compromised. God has a greater vision for you.

Cultivating Hope:

1. Have you ever been stuck in the Glory Days or a Dirge?

2. When have you sensed God was doing a new work in your life?

3. How do you encourage your family and friends to move in a new direction?

Bible Study Questions:

1. How does this truth about new wine relate to us?

"'And no one pours new wine into old wineskins. Otherwise, the new wine will burst the skins; the wine will run out and the wineskins will be ruined. No, new wine must be poured into new wineskins. And no one after drinking old wine wants the new, for they say, "The old is better."'" (Luke 5:37-39)

2. Why is baptism significant, and have you been baptized?

"Then Jesus came from Galilee to the Jordan to be baptized by John. But

John tried to deter him, saying, 'I need to be baptized by you, and do you come to me?'

Jesus replied, 'Let it be so now; it is proper for us to do this to fulfill all righteousness.' Then John consented. 'As soon as Jesus was baptized, he went up out of the water. At that moment heaven was opened, and he saw the Spirit of God descending like a dove and alighting on him. 'And a voice from heaven said, 'This is my Son, whom I love; with him I am well pleased.'" (Matthew 3:13-17)

3. How can you grieve with hope?

"Brothers and sisters, we do not want you to be uninformed about those who sleep in death, so that you do not grieve like the rest of mankind, who have no hope. For we believe that Jesus died and rose again, and so we believe that God will bring with Jesus those who have fallen asleep in him." (1 Thessalonians 4:13-14)

4. How can you embrace the new song God brings?

"Sing to the Lord a new song; sing to the Lord, all the earth. Sing to the Lord, praise his name; proclaim his salvation day after day." (Psalm 96:1-2)

5. What does it look like to trust God?

"'But blessed is the one who trusts in the Lord, whose confidence is in him. They will be like a tree planted by the water that sends out its roots by the stream. It does not fear when heat comes; its leaves are always green. It has no worries in a year of drought and never fails to bear fruit.'" (Jeremiah 17:7-8)

Scan this QR Code to dive deeper with Jesse and watch his video that provides additional stories, insights, and a prayer:

Mend Your Hope

"The thief comes only to steal and kill and destroy; I have come
that they may have life, and have it to the full."
John 10:10

God possesses the power to renew and repair your shattered aspirations and dreams. Jesus stands as the great Healer. While the adversary seeks to pillage, annihilate, and wreak havoc, Jesus enters our lives, offering a bounty of vitality. Grasping both dimensions of this truth is crucial. While an abundant life, replete with a surging hope, is promised and available to us daily, there also exist malevolent entities—hope thieves—that desire to seize, diminish, and obliterate our hope. To truly relish the richness of hope, we must transcend these hope thieves. Let's dive into this analogy, examining these burglars intent on plundering our most cherished treasures and discerning ways to shield and defend our hope.

When you think about your home, if a thief shows up, you would not open the front door and welcome the thief in. You wouldn't leave all the windows and doors open, especially knowing that there are many thieves in the neighborhood. If that thief broke into your house, you wouldn't say, "Oh, can I get you some food?" or "Would you like some coffee or a cup of tea?" You wouldn't ask, "Which chair would you like to sit in? Are you comfortable? Need anything?" or say, "Just make yourself at home!" You wouldn't offer, "Let me show you where I keep my money and valuables. Here's the combination to the safe." You wouldn't tell the thief, "Take whatever you want. Can I help you carry it out? Did you find everything you wanted?" You just wouldn't do that.

In the same way, there are hope thieves who want to take what you have and steal your hope, joy, and peace. If you let them, they will keep taking and taking from you. It's important to identify these thieves and their schemes. With God's help, you can slam the front door, lock the windows, and declare, "Not in my house!"

Let's unmask seven prevalent hope thieves, revealing their true identities and their insidious strategies to infiltrate your life, relations, thoughts, and spirit. Even if only a couple currently threaten your peace, it's essential to discern and thwart their advances. Learning their schemes equips you to project and help others, too. Cultivate a robust resistance. Evict these invaders from your sanctuary. Repel the shadows, melancholy, and malevolent spirits. By doing so, you cultivate a culture and environment brimming with hope as you staunchly defend your innermost being. While I employ the metaphor of a household and its intruders, in essence, it's your heart that demands protection. Safeguard your heart, for it is the fountainhead of all you undertake.

By ousting these culprits, you will make space for God's presence. Let Him reside and reign, healing your wounds and recovering the treasures that these hope thieves have stolen.

Guarding Hope

Every day, hope thieves lurk in the shadows, intent on draining your energy and submerging you in despair. They aren't courteous intruders; they don't knock or seek permission to disrupt your journey. As you strive to live in light, truth, hope, and love, these adversaries can strike unexpectedly, jeopardizing your progress. These thieves can manifest as demons, falsehoods, injustices, direct assaults, or even individuals seeking to destabilize and diminish you. Yet, in the face of these adversaries, remember: God's might surpasses all foes and any force that seeks to steal, annihilate, and wreak havoc. Jesus confidently proclaims His mission to bestow upon us a life of abundance. This gift encompasses triumph over these very hope thieves. *The thief comes only to steal and kill and destroy; I have come that they may have life, and have it to the full.* (John 10:10)

Stay vigilant, for these assailants of hope can be crafty, often masquerading as allies or confidants. They infiltrate your daily life, speaking a language laced with deceit. Their tactics are insidious, their allure reminiscent of poison coated in sweet chocolate.

While their allure may initially seem enticing, the repercussions are profound and enduring. These thieves may promise contentment and sustenance, but in reality, they erode your contentment and jeopardize your future. Recognizing and understanding their strategies is the first step to fortifying your defenses. By doing so, you can reclaim lost hope, shield yourself from future setbacks, and encourage others to rise above. Here's a look at seven prevalent hope thieves and strategies to vanquish them.

Denial: Whether intentional or unintentional, the consequences remain consistent. Choosing to ignore the glaring elephant in the room is a common reaction for many when faced with monumental challenges. While denial might provide a temporary reprieve, it exacerbates the underlying issue over time. It perpetuates a facade of resilience yet offers no genuine solutions. If you suspect you might be in denial, seek honest opinions from those around you. Surround yourself with individuals who care enough to be straightforward with you. When confronted about your denial, avoid getting defensive. Cultivate an environment where others feel safe providing feedback. Embrace the truth, even if it's uncomfortable at first. Real friends give advice that might feel like, "Ouch, that helps!" Denial stifles growth, hampers personal development, ruins relationships, and diminishes hope. Stepping out of denial is akin to leaving a delusional world that stifles hope. Remember, the truth sets you free.

Failure: As a former professional soccer player, certain misplays are etched in my memory. Ideally, I'd erase them, but they occasionally resurface, even in my dreams. One instance that particularly has haunted me involved misjudging a ball. Instead of catching it with my hands, it struck my head and deflected, setting up an easy score for the opposing team. That blunder marked a negative turning point in a particularly challenging season for us. Everyone falters in various aspects of life. Some failures result from taking commendable risks, while others arise from poor judgments. For instance, learning new skills, like snowboarding, inevitably involves wipeouts and mistakes. On my first attempt, I found myself tumbling repeatedly. Other errors, however, stem from ill-advised choices bearing significant consequences.

If not addressed, failures can snowball, affecting one's self-perception, relationships, faith, and future prospects. If you do not put limits on failure, it will put limits on you. Notice I didn't say stop failing, but I said to be proactive and not give failure too much power. I miss the mark every single day. When you fail, remind yourself it is part of learning.

The term "sin" in archery denotes "missing the mark." When we stray from God's teachings, acknowledging our transgressions is crucial. Repentance involves a complete reversal, much like executing a U-turn on the road. Redirecting from sin towards the Savior is always a wise move. The antidote to failure is forgiveness. I firmly believe in Jesus' power to absolve our sins and alleviate the burden of remorse. Don't let past mistakes eclipse your identity or breed desolation. Understand that making mistakes doesn't label you a failure. It's crucial to hold firm, embrace forgiveness, and reclaim hope. If apologies or amendments are in order, ensure you make them promptly. Extend your sincere apologies to those you may have inadvertently or deliberately hurt. Then, receive God's grace in full.

Selfishness: If you are full of yourself, you probably lack hope. If we live solely for ourselves, it's time to embrace a larger cause. I believe we are all wonderfully made and uniquely designed in God's image, holding significance, equality, and boundless potential. We can possess these powerful affirmations without becoming self-absorbed. Your personal branding, social media, or website might be impressive, but what about your motives and intentions? Greater hope comes from serving others, listening well, mourning with those in grief, celebrating others' achievements, and being a team player. It's possible that you may be the last to recognize your self-centeredness. Therefore, set up measures to keep a balanced view of yourself. Your time, thoughts, words, and demeanor are telling. I believe that God's goodness and revering God position us correctly. Repentance turns self-centeredness into a fervor for serving. A proper understanding of God paves the way for a healthy self-perception and an overflow of hope. Your vision should go beyond your ascension to the top of the mountain. True success is when everyone reaches the peak together.

Isolation: Isolation has been dubbed the devil's workshop. Remember, isolation is a choice. You have loved ones who cherish you and want to share life's journey with you. Life hinges on relationships, and your life's quality correlates directly with the caliber of your connections. Do your closest friends encourage hope, bring out the best in you, and share your vision and dedication? The friends you select significantly mold the atmosphere and setting of your existence, deeply influencing your path forward. To walk with the wise is to become wise.

Should you have experienced pain before, be wary of erecting barriers around your heart that deter others. We thrive in unity! Hope dwindles when we either befriend the wrong crowd or lack profound, uplifting friendships. Both scenarios can result in feelings of loneliness and seclusion. Make deliberate choices in prayerfully and carefully choosing your friends and nurturing your closest relationships, and you'll see hope flourish.

Throughout the pandemic, arranging intentional Zoom calls fostered the growth of my relationships with friends and family. We became more purposeful. When you treasure shared moments, you prioritize them. Anticipating our next meet-up became a regular joy. Both utilize the capabilities of technology and be proactive and meet face-to-face (in person is always ideal but not always possible). Take someone out to lunch. Open your doors to budding friendships. Life's obstacles can become opportunities for deeper connections. Invest in your healthiest relationships; they are gifts from God filled with immense hope.

Distraction: We live in a society constantly inundated with negative messages, empty propositions, scams, dead ends, and nonsense. Dozens of individuals have informed me that they've received texts or emails from someone pretending to be me, soliciting money and gift cards. It's very frustrating! Have you noticed how easy it is to pick up your phone, check out your social media feed, and fall into some empty vortex for hours? How often do you set your phone down to engage with people you love? How do you sort through all the negative noise and keep your focus daily? Sometimes, what is good can distract us from what is best. These are important questions and considerations for our minds, hearts, and souls.

Distracted individuals rarely harbor hope. What are your objectives, methodologies, and strategies? Here's a constructive task: pinpoint the three most prominent distractions in your life and devise a plan to overcome them. It's commonly stated: "Either make excuses or create a plan." I sincerely advocate for a distraction plan that facilitates a resurgence of hope and a departure from a defeatist mindset. For the past seven years, our church community has consciously embarked on a three-week fast every January. This ritual has proven invaluable in decluttering, recalibrating, and discerning the non-essentials. Prioritize eradicating unproductive efforts; your time is an invaluable asset.

Negativity: How frequently do you find yourself complaining? When are you besieged by envy or jealousy? Have you ever been plagued by a prideful and judgmental attitude, always presuming the worst? Aspire to be a reconciler, not a disruptor. There's a remarkable story where God emancipated the Israelites from oppression, aiming to usher them into the Promised Land. While contemplating their choices, only Caleb and Joshua, two out of twelve leaders, were poised to embrace the coveted future. The remaining ten leaders exuded pessimism, causing a whole generation to languish in stagnation. Advancement demands bravery, and progress is often polarizing. Don't anticipate your most prudent decisions to invariably garner unanimous endorsement or the lion's share of support.

I do not want to spend my life traveling in circles because it appears to be safer or more familiar! Do you agree? Growth and development are threatening to people who want to protect the status quo through doubt, fear, and intimidation. Consistently and persistently reject the negative voices and statements, even if they come from your own mind! We need heaven's perspectives, promises, and plans because they are always full of hope. Gratitude and words of affirmation crush negativity.

Worry: It's impossible to worry and be full of hope at the same time. They represent a clear fork in the road; you simply can't have both. Worrying stems from trying to exert too much control over a situation. Can worrying add any quality or length to your life? Early in my ministry, I had a wise assistant nearing retirement named Sue. She would often tell me, "Don't go borrowing trouble from tomorrow!" Worry consumes hope just as our dog, Bella, gobbles up any food that falls from the table during family dinners.

Sometimes, understanding why hope is absent points us directly to an aspect of our lives needing change.

In my life, the best antidote for worry has been worship. Expressing gratitude to God, surrendering burdens, sharing my deepest feelings, and engaging in silent meditation have led to a peace that shields my mind and heart. Growing up, I didn't believe in God and never prayed. I learned to pray during the most challenging times in my life. The God of all hope, the very source of hope, generously replaces our worry, soaked in skepticism and doubt, with His perfect love that dispels fear. I believe prayer is powerful. God's most profound interventions often come when situations are bleakest and we are most prone to worry. It's nearly impossible to praise God and still be consumed by worry. Worship transforms us internally. So, choose to worship God over worry.

Your life, your story, and your hope are invaluable! God's love banishes fear and lies. Defend your mind, heart, and soul from daily attacks by those who wish to steal your hope. Cherish what you hold dear and actively safeguard your hope. Remember, you wouldn't just stand by as a burglar entered your home, show them your valuables, and assist them in hauling them away. Adopt a "not in my house" stance against those aiming to rob you of your hope. Your peace and joy are too precious to let intruders freely take what they wish.

A New Start

I love people, and it pains me to see so many get deceived and cheated. I want the best for you. Here's how to stand strong: replace denial with truth, failure with forgiveness, selfishness with service, isolation with friendships, distractions with plans, negativity with gratitude, and worry with worship. You're not on this journey alone. There's a benevolent God who stands by you, champions your cause, and exchanges your frailty for His might. He protects and provides both through and beyond our endeavors.

"We must accept finite disappointment, but we must never lose infinite hope. Carve a tunnel of hope through the dark mountain of disappointment."
- Dr. Martin Luther King, Jr.

Ejecting these seven hope thieves from your life isn't just about creating a void. Instead, it's about inviting God's presence into that space. Half the battle is removing the negatives, but the ultimate victory is achieved when you usher God and His hope into your life. For someone recovering from alcohol addiction, mere sobriety isn't the end goal. Beyond sobriety, an abundant life includes the choices to connect with others, serve, discover our God-given purpose, abide with Jesus, and experience growth and healing. Evicting negative influences is crucial, but an empty heart risks being invaded again. So, open every corner of your heart to God. This is the essence of a life filled with the Spirit.

My mentor, E.K. Bailey from the Concord Missionary Baptist Church in South Oak Cliff (Dallas area), used to say the Holy Spirit should not just reside but preside over our lives. Granting God full control allows you to experience the Spirit's richness, be filled with hope, and become all God has designed you to be.

The Bible instructs us not to grieve or suppress the Holy Spirit:

"Do not grieve the Holy Spirit of God, with whom you were sealed for the day of redemption. Get rid of all bitterness, rage and anger, brawling and slander, along with every form of malice. Be kind and compassionate to one another, forgiving each other, just as in Christ God forgave you." *(Ephesians 4:30-32)*

It also states:

"Do not get drunk on wine, which leads to debauchery. Instead, be filled with the Spirit." (Ephesians 5:18)

And, "'If you then, though you are evil, know how to give good gifts to your children, how much more will your Father in heaven give the Holy Spirit to those who ask him!'" (Luke 11:13)

The essence of Christian life isn't about relying on personal might or wisdom; that would always fall short. We are not self-sufficient. We can't save ourselves. It's about depending on the guidance provided by the scriptures. As we trust God's Spirit, our souls are overflowing with His Spirit and hope. We cannot do this independently. Self-absorption is empty, and so is the idea of a hope-filled life without God's presence. By eliminating negative influences, you create space for God. The Holy Spirit comforts, leads, and empowers you, transforming your life and providing a fountain of everlasting, intimate, and unbreakable hope, for that's the promise of Jesus. I realize this step might be new for you. We step off the throne, and God becomes the leader of our lives. We are active but walk humbly with our Maker.

Truth Over Lies

We're setting the stage for *The Power of the Second Thought*. I have been presenting the overall context and establishing a solid foundation before I present the new tool and habit that will be the focus of subsequent chapters. I appreciate your patience throughout this process. God desires to heal our lives with His love and truth. The Bible clearly states that Jesus embodies truth.

"Jesus answered, 'I am the way and the truth and the life. No one comes to the Father except through me.'" (John 14:6)

The word of God stands as the truth, and it serves as our primary source of truth. Recognizing your source of truth in life is pivotal. It's a decision rooted in faith. What can you always consider accurate, dependable, and trustworthy? We instinctively seek truth, requiring both a moral and spiritual compass. Your primary source of truth could be your intuition, education, emotions, parental advice, cultural norms, prevalent trends, traditional beliefs, or God's word.

While there's a portion of truth in many of those options, falsehoods also lurk in each, with the exception of Scripture. God blesses us with intuition, conscience, and sensible friends. These gifts carry truth but not the whole truth. They lack the unwavering reliability of complete truth. Our hearts can be misleading, emotions deceptive, motives questionable, perspectives limited, friends' advice imperfect, and societal norms can push us into paths diverging from God's directives. God's word rejuvenates our thoughts. While culture represents collective thoughts and ways, scriptures articulate God's thoughts and paths. We must turn to God's word and embrace Jesus for undiluted truth. You will often be at the crossroads of the patterns of the world and the wisdom of the Word.

The devil, as described in the Bible, is the architect of lies. Deception is his forte.

"You belong to your Father, the devil, and you wish to fulfill your Father's desires. He was a murderer from the beginning, not adhering to the truth, as there's no truth in him. When he speaks falsehoods, he's simply expressing his innate nature, for he's a liar, the progenitor of lies." (John 8:44)

This is the misinformation he distributes. Our lives are a daily tug-of-war between truth and deceit, light and shadow, virtue and vice, God and the devil.

This ongoing battle directly impacts our hope. The level of our hope correlates with the volume of truth we accept and the extent of falsehoods we embrace. By discerning the lies that diminish hope, you can replace them with truths that bolster it. Now, I'll outline specific misconceptions about "hope" that you should recognize, dispel, and replace. The strategy with any lie is to identify, expose, eliminate, and then substitute. I want to share three lies about "hope" with you so that you can reject them and replace them with truths.

Lie #1: *Hope is just an unpredictable feeling that comes and goes.*

Feelings are important, legitimate, and play a crucial role in our lives. They are not inherently negative. There's a proper place for feelings in our lives. We shouldn't allow feelings to dictate our every action or decision. Conversely, we shouldn't suppress or ignore them either. Feelings accompany us on our life journey. They're a gift from God but should be balanced with wisdom and discernment. Hope extends beyond mere emotions. While it's essential not to neglect or exaggerate our feelings, hope is fundamentally anchored in facts, not fleeting sensations. Today's world often promotes instant gratification, urging us to seek temporary pleasures without considering the long-term consequences. For many, the quest for immediate satisfaction determines their choices and lifestyles. Such an approach, however, is shortsighted and unfulfilling.

True hope rests on undeniable facts, complemented by faith, which leads to genuine and uplifting emotions. But the emotions themselves shouldn't be the primary concern. The emphasis should be on maintaining a close relationship with God and grounding oneself in facts and truth. While emotions might fluctuate, hope remains steadfast. It's essential to prioritize God and truth over transient feelings. You don't find joy by focusing on joy. Joy comes when you abide with the One who created joy.

Hope is not always predictable. It's relational, always accessible, and can be cultivated since it's also habitual. Recognizing the genuine nature of hope ensures we don't feel lonely or powerless. Hope doesn't sporadically appear or vanish from our lives. It's not a volatile emotion. Let's define hope. At its core, **hope signifies a deep and joyful trust in someone or something**. Its strength correlates with the reliability of its source. Your hope is as strong as the one you trust. Given God's unwavering fidelity, hope emerges as a beacon that is always available. This realization helps us understand that hope isn't a fleeting emotion but provided by God as a personal, eternal, and indestructible gift to receive.

Lie #2: *You will always be stuck with only experiencing a small amount of hope.*

Many people think, *Others might have hope for reasons A, B, and C, but I'll never possess that hope. I've never had it, and I never will.* This is a misconception, a self-imposed barrier. We aim to dispel this notion. God offers a breakthrough. A generation once wandered in the wilderness for 40 years, trapped in an unending cycle. Though God had promised them land, their disbelief kept them from embracing His promise. Similarly, many today find themselves trapped in negative cycles, mistakenly believing they can never experience true hope. How many silently struggle with frustration and anxiety, searching for hope but looking in all the wrong places?

How many invest their resources only to realize they've been pursuing false hopes? How many accept this limiting belief, resigning themselves to a life of mediocrity? Social media often masks these struggles, as people primarily showcase their highlights. But beneath the surface, many believe hope is beyond their reach. If you view hope as fleeting and base it on false foundations, you'll feel trapped, believing that your situation and amount of hope are unchangeable. God doesn't have a low ceiling for your hope.

I'm not suggesting that walking with God is easy or that cultivating new habits is straightforward. But I emphasize that hope is accessible to everyone, and it's richer and more abundant than many realize. God's grace is transformative. So, don't confine yourself to limited hope or perpetually think small. It's time to divorce small thinking and keeping hope in small, bogus boxes. Choose to reawaken rather than resign. Embrace the refreshing truth and transition from a mindset of hope scarcity to the expansive perspective of and power of Jesus.

Lie #3: *There's a person who can bring you all the hope you need.*

Many single individuals believe marriage is the key to a perfect and fulfilling life. They think, *Once I get married, everything will fall into place, and I'll finally find contentment and abundant hope.* I knew I had unrealistic expectations. While marriage is indeed a beautiful gift from God and is the closest human relationship, no individual can fulfill all your hopes or meet your deepest needs. Relying solely on another person for your happiness and contentment can lead to unrealistic expectations and inevitable disappointments. Marriage is relational, intellectual, emotional, physical, spiritual, and wonderful. Never let your greatest blessings become idols. Only Jesus can provide the enduring hope that truly satisfies the soul.

Unspoken expectations in relationships can be harmful, and setting the bar unrealistically high can lead to profound disillusionment, frustration, and even despair. Many believe finding and marrying the "right" person will bring them ultimate contentment. But it's vital to understand that no individual can entirely fulfill you. While marriage is a blessing, it isn't designed to meet your soul's deepest desires. I remained single until my thirties, expecting to marry in my twenties. I eventually married at 34, realizing in hindsight that God had a different timeline and a better plan. Throughout my single years, I waited and prayed, and going deeper with God prepared me more than anything else for marriage. My wife, Laurie, is everything I hoped for, but I never want to burden her with the unrealistic expectation of being my primary source of joy and contentment.

I recognize that only God can meet Laurie's deepest needs and offer her profound hope. There's a liberating feeling when you don't look to another person as your primary hope source. Our marriage thrives most when our love for God surpasses our love for each other. It may sound unconventional, but placing a person above God can deplete hope. This can happen in friendships and dating, too. No one should bear the responsibility of being the primary provider of another's happiness or hope. When God leads a marriage, both partners can draw from Jesus, ensuring a reservoir of hope to share and receive in the relationship. Abiding with God reduces stress, brings peace, not pressure, and alleviates worries and insecurities.

Your Reset

It may be time to reconsider your beliefs and expectations about hope. Silent and unrealistic expectations can be dangerous, often resulting in unnecessary disappointment. As you recalibrate your expectations, align them with the truths that heal, particularly those rooted in grace and God's Word. Embracing truth allows you to receive abundant hope from God. The shifts I refer to involve moving from falsehoods to truths. Hope and truth always reside together.

Transitioning from a lie to the truth involves repentance, allowing hope to flood your life as you make space for God. This transition is compelling, moving you from stagnation and destruction to life that is truly vibrant. Turning from sin towards God restores you. Embracing the light after leaving behind darkness transforms you into the person God designed in His image.

In this section, we have highlighted hope truths, which involve recognizing the lies, eliminating them, repenting, and turning towards God for renewal. Each of these steps creates space for God in your life. Whether it's adopting a new song over dwelling in past glories or exchanging truth for falsehoods, you're making space for both God and hope.

You are opening doors for hope when you expel the hope thieves and grant God full access to your life, inviting the Holy Spirit to reside and preside. Sometimes, our ingrained thought patterns hinder the work and hope of God. Recognize that hope is God's profound work within us. Hope is relational. We've delved into the nuances of abiding. It's often counter-cultural and counter-intuitive, too. Now, we're poised to take action, empowered by the

Holy Spirit. Remember, God accompanies you on this journey, guiding you towards the unwavering hope He offers. God is with you. God is for you. God is good. God has a plan. God never runs out of hope. With that foundation, it's time to focus on *The Power of the Second Thought* and learn a transformative new habit.

Cultivating Hope:

1. Which hope thieves have been active in your life?

2. When have you replaced a destructive lie with an inspiring truth?

3. How can you make room to receive more hope?

Bible Study Questions:

1. How does God help us in the spiritual battle?

"In addition to all this, take up the shield of faith, with which you can extinguish all the flaming arrows of the evil one. Take the helmet of salvation and the sword of the Spirit, which is the word of God. And pray in the Spirit on all occasions with all kinds of prayers and requests. With this in mind, be alert and always keep on praying for all the Lord's people." (Ephesians 6:14-18)

2. How does repentance bring healing and hope?

"If we claim to be without sin, we deceive ourselves, and the truth is not in us. If we confess our sins, he is faithful and just and will forgive us our sins and purify us from all unrighteousness." (1 John 1:8-9)

3. What does it mean that Jesus is the truth?

"To the Jews who had believed him, Jesus said, 'If you hold to my

---

teaching, you are really my disciples. Then you will know the truth, and the truth will set you free.'" (John 8:31-32)

4. What lies do you want to reject?

"You belong to your father, the devil, and you want to carry out your father's desires. He was a murderer from the beginning, not holding to the truth, for there is no truth in him. When he lies, he speaks his native language, for he is a liar and the father of lies. Yet because I tell the truth, you do not believe me!" (John 8:44-45)

5. Why is there hope in God's presence?

"Taste and see that the Lord is good; blessed is the one who takes refuge in him." (Psalm 34:8)

Scan this QR Code to dive deeper with Jesse and watch his video that provides additional stories, insights, and a prayer:

ELEMENT 2: DISCOVER

A New Trust

Hope is a confident and joyful trust in someone or something, and God leads us to discover His indestructible hope. As your desire for hope grows, more becomes available to you. You must discover that hope is both relational and habitual. These are complementary concepts, not competing ones. The relational aspect is foundational, and the habitual empowers you to flourish.

This section aims to guide you through reflections on your faith and relationship with God. I want to provide some background on my life before the tragedy in Africa. I never trusted God. I didn't believe He existed. I didn't grow up following Jesus, attending church, or reading the Bible. My knowledge about God was minimal, and my interest even less. I identified as an atheist. I recall moments in high school, driving with my dad, openly declaring to my friends my belief that there was no God. My family's spiritual beliefs vary; think of it like Baskin-Robbins™ with 31 flavors. While our views diverge widely, our love and respect for each other remain intact.

I recognize that everyone reading has a unique story and distinct perspective. You might harbor significant doubts about God and may consider skipping some of the more spiritual sections of this book. Thank you for being willing to consider the content I share. Perhaps you're exploring faith and spirituality for the first time, finding certain parts of this book challenging to grasp. Maybe you know God, but you're so caught up in your goals and daily activities that you long to reconnect with God. Or, you might be deeply committed with your faith, eager to dive deeper into all that God promises. Whether you're doubting, discovering, distracted, or devoted— hope is for everyone! I'm grateful you are willing to explore your faith alongside me in this narrative. Faith is very personal, and I'm honored we can consider its significance together.

My Faith Journey

My parents divorced when I was seven years old. Watching that unfold was extremely difficult, and I vividly remember the day my dad left. The foundational pillars of my family divided, and I felt powerless to mend or hold our family together. This experience, which was beyond my control, left a profound void in my life. While I harbor no resentment or bitterness towards my parents long ago, this change undeniably shaped my future.

In the aftermath, without knowledge of or inclination toward God, I honed my focus on what I term the "Big Three" priorities—school, sports, and friendships. I operated at that time under the belief that if I excelled in these areas, I'd likely be happy overall. My parents' disintegrating relationship was something I couldn't influence, but these three areas felt more within my abilities. Though I consulted a few counselors, those sessions didn't provide the solace or guidance I sought.

I want to emphasize that counselors can be invaluable. There's absolutely no shame in seeking professional help. I have seen so much healing in countless lives through counselors. Unfortunately, my experience at that time wasn't fruitful. The counselor, in my view, sometimes lacked compassion and understanding, making me feel judged. Yet, with my "Big Three" domains flourishing, I managed to push through without feeling too derailed. Perhaps you can relate? Have you ever leaned heavily on certain successes to bolster your self-worth, especially when confronting painful or overwhelming circumstances?

After graduating from high school, I enrolled at Dartmouth College on the East Coast. Outwardly, my life seemed like a success story. I was attending an Ivy League college and excelling academically. Our soccer team clinched the conference title in my freshman year, and I was recognized with personal accolades. My social calendar was brimming, including joining a fraternity with constant parties. Yet, even with these accomplishments, a gnawing emptiness persisted. If all boxes were checked and goals attained, why did I feel like something was missing? This dissonance hinted that perhaps life held more than the confines I had set for myself.

Two Stories

There are two stories in everyone's life—the outside story and the inside story. The outside story is what people see and perceive. Often, we craft this narrative on social media, ensuring it appears as flawless as possible. Seeing only this facade, most people gain an incomplete understanding of who we truly are. Contrarily, the inside story is the one only we and, more comprehensively, God, understand. While we possess a keen self-awareness, God's comprehension of us is perfect and complete. Reflect on Psalm 139 and marvel at the depth to which you are known and cherished. Some people may know you without truly loving you, while others love you without fully understanding you. However, to be both loved and comprehended deeply is profoundly powerful. God offers this dual intimacy flawlessly. Jesus, often referred to as the Good Shepherd, cherishes you deeply. With Him, no pretense is needed. The interior narrative is always more impactful than the exterior one.

For me, while the exterior seemed bursting with achievements, the interior felt empty. I grappled with identifying anything or anyone who could fill that void. During my freshman year, I enrolled in an "Introduction to World Religions" course. Contrary to what one might assume, a quest for spiritual understanding didn't drive my decision. In fact, I didn't believe in

God and certainly wasn't seeking Him. My sole motive for selecting that course was to fulfill the general requirements that would move me closer to my undergraduate degree.

Facts Lead to Faith

When I enrolled in that class, we studied various religions, analyzing their texts and beliefs. The professor, not a Christian himself, occasionally seemed to try to undermine the Bible. However, our study of the Gospel of John was transformative for me. Unlike any other scripture or text I had read before, the Bible was powerful and felt supernatural, with Jesus as its focal point. As I dove deeper into Jesus's life, though my initial aim was merely academic excellence, I found myself learning about the very personal Savior.

Several aspects made Jesus stand out. First, the Bible, with its extensive circulation and popularity throughout history, highlighted Jesus as an unparalleled teacher, with many regarding him as history's greatest. Second, His miracles, such as walking on water, feeding the masses, healing the blind, and resurrecting Lazarus, among many others, marked Him as unrivaled.

Furthermore, Jesus's claim of sinlessness distinguishes him. While all humans have faltered, succumbing to temptations and deviating from God's path, Jesus remains the sole exception. His impeccable nature, free from sin despite facing temptations, further cements His divinity. We would never revere Jesus if He wasn't the epitome of holiness, perfection, and purity. Additionally, He is unique in being both fully human and fully God.

This duality, while paradoxical, is intrinsic to our faith. Jesus's sacrifice on the cross, substitutionary atonement, includes Him taking our place as a sinless human, enduring crucifixion for our transgressions. This act led to a profound exchange: Jesus bestowed His righteousness upon us, bearing our sins upon the cross. His resurrection, three days post-burial, marked his victory over death. While other religious leaders remain in the grave, Jesus rose. He also promises a return, asserting he will govern as the King of Kings and Lord of Lords, bringing forth a new heaven and earth for eternity.

Relationship Over Religion

Clearly, Jesus had captured my interest. Though He hadn't won my heart or loyalty yet, he had sparked my curiosity. Recognizing that trust forms the foundation of all relationships, including one with God, I felt compelled to explore further. When I impartially examined Christianity in relation to other religions and belief systems, I noticed two distinct features about Christianity that made it unique.

First, Christianity emphasized a relationship with God rather than a mere adherence to rituals, rules, or traditional religion. It was a bond with the living God. Second, the concept of grace was uniquely powerful and profound. Widely celebrated in the spiritual classic "Amazing Grace," this unmerited favor represents a gift that, though freely given to us, came at an unimaginable cost to Jesus. By placing trust in Him, one receives the complete forgiveness of sins, eternal life, and a secured place in God's everlasting family. This isn't about our accomplishments but Christ's sacrifice for us.

God's pursuit of me, His intimate knowledge and love for me before I even acknowledged Him, deeply resonated. Such truths remain constant, regardless of our acceptance or rejection. While we have an idea of how to respond to His generous offer, it became a matter of trust for me. Yet, I was still in a phase of exploration, gathering more insights and being gradually drawn by His grace. Recognizing that His benevolence often leads us to repentance, I acknowledged Jesus's love, demonstrated in words and through His selfless actions. It stood out that Jesus claimed to be the Messiah. That's a bold claim, and it's worthy of our time and investigation. I wanted to find historical evidence for faith. So, I learned more about the Bible and its reliability.

Trust is Core

First and foremost, the Bible stands out because of its claims to be the word of God and its assertion of truthfulness. Comparing the number of copies, their accuracy, and how closely they date back to the original text, the Bible surpasses many historical texts we typically accept as trustworthy. The practical applicability of the Bible, as well as its ability to transform when genuinely lived, further influenced my perspective. I read the Bible, and I was reading the lives of Christians I encountered, noticing in them something I lacked.

Furthermore, the overwhelming evidence for Jesus's resurrection and the fact that His tomb remains empty is undeniable; no one has ever found Jesus's body. It's intriguing that women were the first to witness the resurrected Christ. In that era, women sadly were often perceived as inferior, but God does not share this perspective. He values men and women equally, and His decision to reveal Himself to women first is notable. Other compelling pieces of evidence include the testimonies of over 500 witnesses, the profound life transformations of the Apostle Paul and the disciples, and their unwavering willingness to die for their belief in the resurrection. While people might willingly die for a cause they believe in, it's improbable for them to lay down their lives for a known lie. The journeys of the disciples align with their accounts of witnessing the resurrected Christ.

This accumulation of evidence was vital for my faith, as growing in a relationship with God involves the mind, heart, and soul. God engaged all aspects in me. Evaluating faith is similar to being a jury member, examining all available evidence before making a well-informed decision based on what seems most probable. Through this journey, God broke down my defenses and softened my heart.

As I explored faith throughout the year, I simply prayed, "Jesus, show me who you truly are." It's astonishing how much God reveals when we are receptive. It's all too common to shut ourselves off, often due to past pains, encounters with hypocritical individuals, or disappointments with those labeling themselves as Christian. However, God presents Himself to those who seek, those who remain open, and those with a spiritual hunger. Those who genuinely thirst for righteousness will be satisfied. Many have claimed the title of God's son over the centuries, but only One has living water to satisfy the soul.

C.S. Lewis, in his work *Mere Christianity,* notes that when someone claims they are the Messiah, there are only three intellectual responses: they are either Lord, a liar, or a lunatic. They're either deluded, believing they are the Messiah; deceitful, claiming a falsehood knowingly; or they genuinely are the Savior of the world. Faced with these options, I realized a decision was imperative. To me, Jesus is exactly who He claims to be, and there is no greater hope to be found than in Him.

I'd like to mention that throughout this year-long process of introspection, and even before that, I constantly gave God "the Heisman." I adopted a stance of "no, thanks," pushing Him away and essentially signaling Him to keep His distance. It required me to let go of my pride, my sense of self-sufficiency, and my doubts, especially as the facts became undeniably clear. I had to abandon my idols and my attempts to structure life around three main areas I believed I could control and excel in. Undergoing such shifts is a humbling experience. Don't let such transitions deter or intimidate you from progressing. I mention this because many people are stubbornly neglecting the most abundant source of hope. The hope you possess will never exceed what your chosen source can offer. We need more than just human-originated hope. My spiritual journey resonates with Jeremiah 2:13:

"My people have committed two sins: They have forsaken me, the spring of living water, and have dug their own cisterns, broken cisterns that cannot hold water."

I had broken cisterns instead of living water. Jesus asked powerful questions, and the one in Mark 8:36 got me:

> *"What good is it for someone to gain the whole world, yet forfeit their soul?"*

A Safe Place

God might place someone in your life specifically to guide you. Maybe you sense God's presence now as you are reading. For me, that person was Mike, who lived in my dormitory. Mike was from a small town in Tennessee and a devout follower of Jesus. He patiently provided a safe space for me throughout that year, fielding my numerous questions—probably over a hundred of them. Everyone requires a positive and uplifting environment where they can unpack their doubts, beliefs, and the reasons underlying those convictions. This is where Mike came in, addressing my questions to the best of his ability. If he was unsure, he'd introduce me to his friend, Brian. I never felt judged or looked down upon by either of them. They were beacons of hope in a world that had often left me wanting.

Perhaps your past encounters with faith were marred by hypocrisy, unkindness, or disillusionment from a church experience. It's crucial to have environments where you can freely discover faith, gather knowledge, and make informed decisions. There's no bond more vital than the one with God, our ultimate source of hope. As we grow closer to Him, our hope multiplies. If you pursue hope, you might find some more of it, but ultimately, it will usher you toward God. Seek God, and you'll be bestowed with boundless hope. Prioritize Him in all aspects of life to receive unwavering hope. As Romans 15:13 states:

> *"May the God of hope fill you with all joy and peace as you trust in Him, so that you may overflow with hope by the power of the Holy Spirit."*

God—comprising the Father, Son, and Holy Spirit—eagerly wants to fill your life with hope. A crucial aspect of unearthing profound hope is cultivating and enjoying a deeper walk with God. John 3:16, probably the Bible's most famed verse, says:

"For God so loved the world that He gave his one and only Son, that whoever believes in Him shall not perish but have eternal life."

This is God's open invitation. You can always grow deeper with God. Knowing Jesus is a pivotal, personal decision, mirroring the commitment of marriage. You can consider this covenant relationship but eventually, you finalize your choice, entering a forever relationship of unparalleled security and hope. Such a covenant with God assures you of His eternal promises. Faith in Jesus is also like the decision to trust a chair when you sit on it, confident that it'll bear your weight. Similarly, embracing Jesus means placing your complete trust in Him, and receiving His grace. Your spiritual life is the story of the condition of your soul. What is more important than your soul?

Love and Hope

God gives you a new identity and the strongest affirmations. Diving deeper into your identity in Christ, you'll find an inexhaustible reservoir of hope. Recognizing God's true nature allows you to perceive the depth of love He holds for you. Understanding that God crafted you with intention and unwavering love means realizing you're destined to be showered with His grace and affirmations. When Jesus emerged from the waters of baptism, the Father proclaimed:

"This is my Son, whom I love; with Him I am well pleased." (Matthew 3:17)

The Bible emphasizes that the love God has for Jesus mirrors the love He has for you. Faith, hope, and love intricately intertwine, forming a resilient cord. By acknowledging and embracing His promises and affirmations, you find renewed purpose, stepping into the grand design He envisioned for you. The Scriptures overflow with these affirmations and promises meant for you. God's word, living and active, holds transformative power.

In the Appendix, I've curated a selection of these powerful affirmations for your reflection. Delve deep into this wellspring of hope. Dedicate time to meditate on these scriptures, allowing them to dwell in you richly just like you enjoy your favorite meals. I urge you to invest time each day, absorbing more of these hope-filled words and affirmations from God. The promises of God bring rest to anyone who is weary of wavering.

Let these verses land deeply in your soul. They are more than precepts and facts; they lead you to God and help you walk in love and truth. Without promises, hope wanders and fades. Facts pave the path to faith, and our faith journey typically follows this sequence: facts lead to faith, which then evokes feelings. Aligning with God means embracing truth—a truth that is saturated with love. This truth encompasses your heart, mind, soul, and strength. Hope, sourced from the God of hope, is the epitome of relational connections. Moreover, hope is habitual.

I emphasize this relationship with God because it forms the bedrock of your hope. It's evident that without a robust foundation, constructing anything becomes challenging. Jesus, our steadfast Rock, invites us to construct our lives upon Him. It's essential to abide with Him. While hope is readily accessible and inherently relational, it's also habitual. Let's further explore this facet of hope and discover a new tool that renews your mind.

Cultivating Hope:

1. How would you describe your faith journey?

2. In what ways would you like to grow spiritually?

3. How is hope relational?

Bible Study Questions:

1. How does Lydia discover hope?

"On the Sabbath, we went outside the city gate to the river, where we expected to find a place of prayer. We sat down and began to speak to the women who had gathered there. One of those listening was a woman from the city of Thyatira named Lydia, a dealer in purple cloth. She was a worshiper of God. The Lord opened her heart to respond to Paul's message. When she and the members of her household were baptized, she invited us to her home. 'If you consider me a believer in the Lord," she said, "come and stay at my house.' And she persuaded us." (Acts 16:13-15)

2. What inspires you about Paul's story of hope?

"Here is a trustworthy saying that deserves full acceptance: Christ Jesus came into the world to save sinners—of whom I am the worst. But for that very reason I was shown mercy so that in me, the worst of sinners, Christ Jesus might display his immense patience as an example for those who would believe in him and receive eternal life. Now to the King eternal, immortal, invisible, the only God, be honor and glory for ever and ever. Amen." (1 Timothy 1:15-17)

3. In what ways does the resurrection impact Mary and us?

Now Mary stood outside the tomb crying. As she wept, she bent over to look into the tomb and saw two angels in white, seated where Jesus' body had been, one at the head and the other at the foot. They asked her, "Woman, why are you crying?"

"They have taken my Lord away," she said, "and I don't know where they have put him." At this, she turned around and saw Jesus standing there, but she did not realize that it was Jesus.

He asked her, "Woman, why are you crying? Who is it you are looking for?"

Thinking he was the gardener, she said, "Sir, if you have carried him away, tell me where you have put him, and I will get him."

Jesus said to her, "Mary."

She turned toward him and cried out in Aramaic, "Rabboni!" (Which means "Teacher"). (John 20:11-16)

4. How does God transform families?

"Suddenly, there was such a violent earthquake that the foundations of the prison were shaken. At once, all the prison doors flew open, and everyone's chains came loose. The jailer woke up, and when he saw the prison doors open, he drew his sword and was about to kill himself because he thought the prisoners had escaped. But Paul shouted, "Don't harm yourself! We are all here!"

The jailer called for lights, rushed in, and fell trembling before Paul and Silas. He then brought them out and asked, "Sirs, what must I do to be saved?"

They replied, "Believe in the Lord Jesus, and you will be saved—you and your household." Then they spoke the word of the Lord to him and to all the others in his house. At that hour of the night the jailer took them and washed their wounds; then immediately he and all his household were baptized. The jailer brought them into his house and set a meal before them; he was filled with joy because he had come to believe in God—he and his whole household." (Acts 16:26-34)

5. How does God reach skeptics?

Now Thomas (also known as Didymus[a]), one of the Twelve, was not with the disciples when Jesus came. So the other disciples told him, "We have seen the Lord!"

But he said to them, "Unless I see the nail marks in his hands and put my finger where the nails were, and put my hand into his side, I will not believe."

A week later, his disciples were in the house again, and Thomas was with them. Though the doors were locked, Jesus came and stood among them and said, "Peace be with you!" Then he said to Thomas, "Put your finger here; see my hands. Reach out your hand and put it into my side. Stop doubting and believe."

Thomas said to him, "My Lord and my God!"

Then Jesus told him, "Because you have seen me, you have believed; blessed are those who have not seen and yet have believed." (John 20:24-29)

Scan this QR Code to dive deeper with Jesse and watch his video that provides additional stories, insights, and a prayer:

A New Tool

*"Finally, brothers and sisters, whatever is true, whatever is noble,
whatever is right, whatever is pure, whatever is lovely, whatever
is admirable—if anything is excellent or praiseworthy—
think about such things."*
Philippians 4:8

This scripture encourages us to be intentional and underscores that our thoughts are a matter of choice.

Every day, you have a choice of what you want to focus on, and whatever you focus on will be magnified in your life. Also, the passage tells us that our thinking needs to be positive and proactive. Instead of indiscriminately latching onto every fleeting thought, It's important to guide your thinking. Moreover, this passage suggests that our thoughts can be infused with hope.

I urge you to utilize this tool, consciously making thought choices that are not only intentional but also full of hope. So how does that work? In my recovery from the tragedy in Africa, a primary piece was the battle in my mind. Especially during the first few years of my recovery, my thoughts often veered into a chasm filled with shadows of despair and discouragement. I didn't know any way to deal with it. Do you ever feel like your thoughts are not helpful and want to take you to some dark places?

New Thoughts

I want to introduce to you a concept I call *The Power of the Second Thought*. This hope-fueled habit has been instrumental in my journey, especially in overcoming the tragedy in Africa. According to the National Science Foundation, a staggering 80% of our initial daily thoughts might not be beneficial. Considering such a high percentage, it's vital to actively curate our thoughts throughout the day.

You have a responsibility when it comes to governing your mind. Think of yourself as an air traffic controller, directing which thoughts to allow and which to dismiss. This is a role only you can undertake, though God provides the wisdom and tools to effectively empower you.

"Sow a thought, and you reap an action; sow an act and reap a habit; sow a habit, and you reap a character; sow a character, and you reap a destiny."
- Ralph Waldo Emerson

Psychologists estimate that our daily thought count can range between 6,000 to 60,000, depending on the person and the day. Given that a vast majority of these initial thoughts may not foster hope or productivity, how should we navigate this mental landscape?

Drawing from my experience as a professional goalkeeper, where my job was to prevent soccer balls from reaching the net, I recognized a similar role I needed to play in my mind post-retirement. The objective? To block negative thoughts from landing in my mind. Just as the goalkeeper must be vigilant, agile, and fully engaged, I needed those same qualities in my mental space. Your mind operates like an air traffic control tower, with continual thoughts landing and taking off constantly. Just like planes, your thoughts need direction and oversight.

The mind, in all its complexity, is both a mystery and a marvel, a gift from God with boundless potential. Yet, its operation can be distilled to a simple principle: reject the initial, when negative, thoughts and replace them with a constructive "second thought" to foster healing and growth. This tool is accessible to everyone. You have the ability to guide your thoughts daily, and while you play this active role, God is right there, empowering and encouraging you. If feelings of passivity or victimization dominate your thinking, this approach can be a practical way to reignite your faith and allow God to refresh your mind.

Reject and Replace

I want to share an example of how helpful and practical this tool is with a "second thought." A recurring thought plagued me incessantly during my rehabilitation: *I am never going to improve. My life will never get better. Hope is an illusion.* The frequency and intensity of this thought were overwhelming. The natural tendency with such persistent thoughts is to either accept them as truth or dwell on them, inadvertently allowing them to erode your hope. These intrusive thoughts manifest differently for different people: feelings of worthlessness, unlovability, incompetence, or the belief that closeness with God is unattainable. While we cannot prevent these initial thoughts from appearing, our reaction to them within the subsequent moments is within our control. This tool equips us to discern which thoughts to dismiss and how to counter them with an intentional, constructive "second thought."

This process of redirecting our thought patterns involves substituting negativity with positivity, falsehoods with truths, and despair with authentic hope. The transformative power of redirecting our thoughts is evident in scripture.

"But he said to me, 'My grace is sufficient for you, for my power is made perfect in weakness.' Therefore, I will boast all the more gladly about my weaknesses, so that Christ's power may rest on me. That is why, for Christ's sake, I delight in weaknesses, in insults, in hardships, in persecutions, in difficulties. For when I am weak, then I am strong." (2 Corinthians 12:9-10)

The apostle Paul, amidst his tribulations, sought God's intervention for relief from his "thorn in the flesh." Despite his emotional pleas, his situation remained unchanged. Yet, he discerned a deeper truth: God's power shines brightest in our frailties. Paul clung to God's assurance, "My grace is sufficient for you." This verse became a pillar of strength for me, a constant reminder of God's unwavering grace.

Empowered Daily

When I would be tempted to think, *My life will never get better; there's no hope,* my second thought became, *My grace is sufficient for you.* As often as the discouragement would come, that's how often I would say this new second thought, *My grace is sufficient for you.* Why is that second thought so powerful? Because it reminds me of God's grace, which I can't deny in my life. I became a Christian in college. During the tragedy of my illness, I was a young Christian, a newer Christian. Still, it helped me to remember my journey, how far God had brought me, how much God has done for me, and my secure identity and hope found in God. *The Power of the Second Thought* is rooted in grace. God provides all we need for life and godliness. Don't harbor or accept a narrative of hopelessness: reject and replace.

The Bible is brimming with affirmations that can counteract discouragement and anxieties, propelling one towards gratitude rather than grumbling. Let's go deeper with the phrase that continues to resonate profoundly with me: "My grace is sufficient for you." The phrase "my grace is" served as a daily reminder that God's grace would be ample for each day. There's no merit in being preoccupied with the uncertainties of tomorrow; after all, each day brings its own challenges. While the entirety of my journey remained uncertain, I was grounded in the realization that every day is a divine gift. Uncertainties about my lifespan, potential career paths, or even my capacity to assist others didn't overshadow the core truth: God's grace for today is enough. "He who began a good work is faithful to complete it" is from

Philippians 1:6 and is another phrase that bolstered my faith. This assurance propelled me to a lifestyle of dependence, recognizing that spiritual growth is rooted in reliance. We aren't islands of self-sufficiency; rather, the essence of Jesus's message urges us to persistently "abide" or remain in Him. In fact, He emphasizes this vital connection in John chapter 15, repeating the word "abide" ten times.

Abiding includes *The Power of the Second Thought.* Jesus is the true vine—we are the branches.

"Remain in me, as I also remain in you. No branch can bear fruit by itself; it must remain in the vine. Neither can you bear fruit unless you remain in me. 'I am the vine; you are the branches. If you remain in me and I in you, you will bear much fruit; apart from me you can do nothing.'" (John 15:4-5)

If we abide with Him, we will bear much fruit—not just a little fruit or a moderate amount, but much fruit. Therefore, my number one role each day is to abide with Jesus. If I stay close to Jesus, this is trust, this is relational, this is listening, this is receiving. If I stay close to Him, I will bear much fruit. Jesus will guide our thinking. He gives us His perspective and power. This second thought started to change my life.

The Power of the Second Thought is very practical. If your environment at work is weighing you down, your first thought might be that you will be miserable constantly at work. Now, you might need to change your job at some point. For now, you can hold onto this second thought: *I will choose to be thankful in all situations.* If your children are wearing down your patience and your first thought contains resentment, you can choose a second thought: *My children are an incredible gift.* If you feel like you are worried and anxious about details and outcomes, you can choose a second thought: *God's love drives out my fear.*

Live with Hope

"The very least you can do in your life is figure out what you hope for.
And the most you can do is live inside that hope. Not admire it
from a distance but live right in it, under its roof."
- Barbara Kingsolver, *Animal Dreams*

There was a time when if I overfocused on my problems, my problems would grow. If you stare at your problems too long, your problems will get bigger in your mind, and God will get smaller. But if you put your focus on Jesus, then He's going to be magnified, and your problems are going to take their right size. You will not be in denial, but you will not feed your fears either. Whatever you feed grows. Feed your faith. Feed your mind with the Word of God. If your mind is spiritually starved, it will start sorting through the trash, looking for something to devour. Garbage in, garbage out. Input and output are linked. Meditation can lead to magnification. This second thought is key with internal victories. When I meditate and fill my mind with "My grace is sufficient for you." my mind is renewed. I'm going to thank God for His grace. What you think about internally becomes played out externally. Make good decisions with your thoughts, and there will be much fruit in every other part of your life.

I learned how to focus on the fact that God will be faithful in my life. He's going to keep His promises. When I have my mind focused on Jesus and the promise that His grace is sufficient, I will abide with Jesus.

God might bless you with money. There's nothing wrong with money. It's a blessing. The *love* of money, elevating it above God and other people, is the root of all kinds of evil, but there is nothing wrong with money itself. But when Jesus says you're going to bear much fruit, that doesn't mean you're going to have a big bank account. You can love Jesus and have a little bit of money or a lot of money. That's not the fruit. The Bible says:

"But the fruit of the Spirit is love, joy, peace, forbearance, kindness, goodness, faithfulness, gentleness, and self-control." (Galatians 5:22)

When you abide with Jesus, there's going to be the fruit in your life that is love, joy, and peace. That's when you're going to have the most hope. I want to say it clearly: being close to Jesus will bring the most hope in your life.

Relationally, if you drift and wander, if you reject Him, if you ignore Him, or if you get distracted, there is going to be less hope. Hope has a name, and His name is Jesus. Hope is relational, but hope is also habitual because God gives us tools to empower and encourage us. *The Power of the Second Thought* is added to your toolbox when you choose to cultivate this habit. God will use your new habit to renew your mind. When a smoke detector starts to chirp, it signals that it's time to change the battery. You replace the dead battery with one that has power and purpose. In the same way, take out the dead and destructive thinking and recharge with thoughts that bring hope, truth, love, and life. You will be amazed at the difference this makes in your inner life and how healthy your thinking can become. Inspiration and transformation happen not when you comprehend this new tool but when you start to use it. It works! God will guide you and be there at every turn, leading you with His thoughts and ways. God is faithful, and it's time to learn a new habit and develop some new patterns of thinking.

Cultivating Hope:

1. Do you have a favorite tool you use for work projects?

2. What is *The Power of the Second Thought*?

3. What thoughts would you like to begin to reject?

Bible Study Questions:

1. How does God help you break out of the world's patterns?

"Therefore, I urge you, brothers and sisters, in view of God's mercy, to offer your bodies as a living sacrifice, holy and pleasing to God—this is your true and proper worship. Do not conform to the pattern of this world, but be transformed by the renewing of your mind. Then you will be able to test and approve what God's will is—his good, pleasing and perfect will." (Romans 12:1-2)

2. What is your old self and what are your old ways of thinking?

"You were taught, with regard to your former way of life, to put off your old self, which is being corrupted by its deceitful desires; to be made new in the attitude of your minds; and to put on the new self, created to be like God in true righteousness and holiness.

Therefore each of you must put off falsehood and speak truthfully to your neighbor, for we are all members of one body." (Ephesians 4:22-25)

3. What is the inward renewal God brings?

"Therefore, we do not lose heart. Though outwardly we are wasting away, yet inwardly we are being renewed day by day. For our light and momentary troubles are achieving for us an eternal glory that far outweighs them all. So we fix our eyes not on what is seen, but on what is unseen, since what is seen is temporary, but what is unseen is eternal." (2 Corinthians 4:16-18)

4. How can you abide with Jesus during the day?

"Remain in me, as I also remain in you. No branch can bear fruit by itself; it must remain in the vine. Neither can you bear fruit unless you remain in me."

"I am the vine; you are the branches. If you remain in me and I in you, you will bear much fruit; apart from me you can do nothing." (John 15:4-5)

5. What does it look like to live out this exhortation?

"We demolish arguments and every pretension that sets itself up against the knowledge of God, and we take captive every thought to make it obedient to Christ." (2 Corinthians 10:5)

Scan this QR Code to dive deeper with Jesse and watch his video that provides additional stories, insights, and a prayer:

A New Habit

Why habits? When you start to use your new tool regularly, it becomes a habit. Tools are designed to be used; they have a purpose. Tools are essential for developing habits. Habits are very powerful. They are intentional choices that may initially seem small but lead to massive results due to their repetitive nature. You will begin cultivating these new habits, which will prove to be transformative and life-giving. "Hope habits" are choices that multiply hope. You begin to do consistently what others do only occasionally.

Habits Become Foundational

Any strong house needs a strong foundation. Why do people wait until life crashes before they take the time and effort to form a solid foundation? You can learn early or late. People who learn early are teachable and eager to do what God says. Those who learn late are stubborn and endure extra and unnecessary heartaches, headaches, and scars. Wisdom says: start building the foundation now. Learn early. Without a strong foundation, hope erodes. Growing a stronger foundation enables you to ascend to new heights. There are essential foundational stones or building blocks that produce hope. Habits are vital for your foundation and are often overlooked and undervalued.

People frequently talk about the height, aesthetics, and curb appeal of a structure. The Space Needle in Seattle, the Golden Gate Bridge in San Francisco, the Empire State Building in New York, and the Washington

Monument in Washington, D.C., are all impressive and memorable. While the visual aspects are significant for a completed design, if the foundations are weak or defective, the structures will not stand. Both tangible and invisible foundations exist for homes, office buildings, skyscrapers, careers, marriages, friendships, faith, success, and hope.

Habits are an essential aspect of how hope can be cultivated consistently and daily. Hope habits are designed to help you grow in areas as they become embedded in your routines. God aids everyday people in understanding His indestructible hope in real-life scenarios. Jesus encouraged everyone to take the time to build a sound foundation for their lives. Being a doer of His words includes learning redemptive habits that originate from God. Two thousand years ago, Jesus spoke of this same idea, and the crowds that gathered around Him were captivated by every word, astounded by His wisdom.

"Therefore everyone who hears these words of mine and puts them into practice is like a wise man who built his house on the rock." (Matthew 7:24)

Abiding with Jesus and cultivating hope habits are the difference between a house on the rock and a house on the sand.

Four Stages of Development

How do you use this new tool, *The Power of the Second Thought*? Any habit has four stages of development, and I want to unpack these. I believe they will be encouraging because they offer a realistic picture of establishing a new habit in your life. It's unlikely that you will master this habit in just a few days or weeks. Instead, you will experience a progression. Don't quit; continue to persevere through the process. You will encounter ups and downs as you start utilizing your new tool and become familiar with this habit.

Here's an overview of the four stages of learning and embedding a new habit: unconscious incompetence, conscious incompetence, conscious competence, and finally, unconscious competence.

Growth and development are a process that encompasses stages of learning. Breaking down the steps it takes for us to learn and master something new, like the hope habits discussed in this book, can be beneficial. If you're finding it challenging to master new habits, or if *The Power of the Second Thought* is unfamiliar to you, that's okay. Developing a new habit takes time. I assure you that as you practice more and more, you will be able to harness these habits during key moments throughout the day. They will begin to feel natural. There are four basic learning stages:

1. **Stage One: Unconscious Incompetence** - At this stage, you are unaware of a skill or solution (unconscious), and you haven't acquired the habit (incompetence). In essence, you don't know what you don't know. For instance, as an infant, I was unaware of shoes and couldn't fathom tying one. Some hope habits might be entirely foreign to you, making you unconsciously incompetent. It might be an area of life where you lack training or awareness. However, the journey doesn't end here.

2. **Stage Two: Conscious Incompetence** - This is when you're aware of what you should do (conscious), but you haven't mastered it (incompetence). As I began attempting to tie my shoe, I consistently failed. The loops and knots wouldn't come together. Initially, you might experience this with *The Power of the Second Thought*—giving it your best shot but not quite getting it right. Don't quit or give up during this stage. You might be tempted to go back to old patterns and feel hopeless. Keep learning and practicing your new habit. Be persistent. In this stage, you are closer to a breakthrough than you feel.

3. **Stage Three: Conscious Competence** - Now you can achieve the task (competence), but it requires intense focus and effort (conscious). It's neither easy nor quick. For example, when I managed to tie my shoe, I had to concentrate deeply, free from distractions. At times, I'd have to retie it. Yet, when I finally did, it felt like a victory. Celebrate every milestone, no matter how minor. I recall the painstaking practice from my youth. It demanded my

full attention until, one day, things began to shift. With *The Power of the Second Thought*, you will begin to reject and replace destructive thoughts quicker. It's intentional at first, but it will become more natural with more practice.

4. **Stage Four: Unconscious Competence** - This is the point where the skill becomes second nature. You don't need to think about it (unconscious) and can execute it with excellence (competence). Today, I can tie my shoe effortlessly, multitasking as I do so.

With *The Power of the Second Thought*, this level of proficiency will become automatic. Throughout the day, you'll subconsciously recognize unhelpful thoughts, replacing them with beneficial ones. Your new habit will develop into an instinctive one through time and repetition. You will recognize hope thieves, lies, and destructive thoughts and slam the door shut more quickly. Your mind will know to shift to the second thought that is life-giving, pure, and inspiring.

Set Your Mind

Hope habits also become more automatic over time. As I practiced this habit, I steered my mind away from falsehoods and toward the truth. I replaced discouraging thoughts with encouraging ones. I swapped fear-based ideas for statements that were a catalyst for courage. I removed inaccurate perceptions of myself and replaced them with affirmations of what God says about me.

Just as adjusting a thermostat changes the temperature in a room, altering your thinking with an intentional second thought transforms your inner life and the atmosphere of your mind and heart. With practice, you'll own this habit in an exciting way! Eventually, reaching the stage of unconscious competence, you'll constantly employ *The Power of the Second Thought* in every facet of your life—where you live, work, learn, and play.

Moreover, you'll teach and uplift others, creating a ripple effect. This is far more than just information; the transformation happens in and through you. Remember these four stages and celebrate your progress as you learn how to wield this new tool.

- *Unconscious Incompetence*: You're oblivious to your lack of knowledge or skill.

- *Conscious Incompetence*: You've begun the learning process but haven't mastered the skill yet.

- *Conscious Competence*: You can execute the task but with intense focus and effort. It might feel like you're exerting extra effort, the process is slow, and it demands all your energy.

- *Unconscious Competence*: This is the pinnacle where the skill or habit feels second nature. You execute it seamlessly, almost without thinking, and achieve proficiency. There is an acceleration of progress, and you are able to teach *The Power of the Second Thought* to other people.

Own the Habit

Let me approach the four stages from a different angle, drawing from my passion: being a goalkeeper. Originally, I was a basketball player, dreaming of the NBA. However, my talent unexpectedly emerged in soccer. After watching me play basketball, the soccer coach believed he could mold me into a goalkeeper. At my very first practice, he took me aside and instructed, "Jesse, this is how you catch a soccer ball." Demonstrating with a "W" shape formed by his hands, he continued, "This is the proper technique." Until then, I had existed in the realm of unconscious incompetence. I knew how to catch a basketball, but soccer is a very different sport and skillset.

Initially, his guidance was lost on me. As I attempted to emulate his "W," my attempts were clumsy, never quite aligning with the ball and my hands. This phase was the epitome of conscious incompetence.

Dedication and commitment are crucial when fostering habits. As I spent more time practicing, even sleeping with a soccer ball, my proficiency began to emerge. Gradually, I mastered the "W" technique. In matches, I'd constantly remind myself of that "W." The technique was there, but it felt somewhat forced, consuming a significant portion of my focus. Yet, over time, the "W" became second nature. Whether the ball came at me in a powerful shot, deflection, or a breakaway, I'd catch it effortlessly with a "W." This technique was my newfound tool, a habit that I nurtured through the stages of development.

This skill served me well at every level. In high school, our team clinched the state championship twice. During my junior year, despite having mastered the "W," the intimidating atmosphere of the Metrodome and its 6,000 spectators unnerved me. Fear can be a formidable barrier, even when a habit is deeply ingrained. Although we won the game, my performance was far from my best. However, I learned not to succumb to fear in my senior year. I trusted my fundamentals. The "W" had never failed me, and I wasn't about to let fear disrupt that. You will face trials and stages in life, so relying on your foundational habits is essential. I eagerly anticipated the opportunity to play in another championship game.

Learning from Past Failures

Anytime in life when you're given an opportunity to revisit a previous failure and tackle it anew, it's a precious gift. I continued to trust my training and be proactive instead of reactive. We were back in the same stadium and clinched the state tournament title game in a dramatic shootout. I believe this success paved the way for my college career and opportunities to play at higher levels. In college, our team reached the NCAA Division 1 Elite Eight. This triumphant journey featured a thrilling shootout victory against our arch-rivals in the tournament. The "W" technique held its ground even in the most high-pressure games. A good habit will be tested in the trials of life. When it makes a difference, your confidence in the habit grows.

This technique served me well overseas, both in Scotland and Africa. My point is certain habits transcend age, life stage, and environment. They're universally effective. For a goalkeeper, catching the ball with the "W" technique works on any soccer field, anywhere in the world. Similarly, in life, inspiring and redemptive habits work in every location. Replacing unhelpful thoughts will be fruitful regardless of whether things are going as desired or if you're navigating a challenging phase. When applied consistently, it allows God to renew your mind. Now, I want to share with you an example of *The Power of the Second Thought* and the difference it made in my life where I initially struggled. I never thought I would need to learn how to drive again in my twenties.

New Breakthroughs

I've just touched on some of my soccer highlights, but now I want to share with you a low point. This one isn't related to sports but to driving. It was, to be candid, a period marked by shame and humiliation. During the years of my recovery, I lost the ability to drive. My heart, physically, had become so sensitive that the slightest stimulation, like a car passing by, would send my heart rate skyrocketing. With my heart prone to arrhythmia, driving was simply too risky. For the first year, it made sense for me not to drive as I needed time to recover. I was waiting for my heart rate and heart rhythms to return to the normal range.

However, even as my heart began to stabilize, my mind continued to battle panic attacks. Despite fewer episodes of an elevated heart rate, relearning how to drive calmly was an ordeal. I recall one short drive to McDonald's, barely a mile away. While waiting in the drive-through for ice cream, a panic attack overcame me. The journey back home, with my heart pounding fiercely, left me wondering if I'd ever drive normally again. Past traumas and failures can profoundly affect our thoughts, often snuffing out hope.

I came to understand that I lacked a mental strategy when driving. My mind would get trapped in a vortex of self-doubt: *What if I can't do this? What if my heart rate soars? What if I have a panic attack?* Old memories of failed driving attempts would replay, gnawing at my confidence and capability. To combat this, I found solace in Isaiah 41:10, which became my new guiding thought:

> *"So do not fear, for I am with you; do not be dismayed, for I am your God. I will strengthen you and help you; I will uphold you with my righteous right hand."*

This verse from Isaiah offers a sense of comfort and assurance. While driving, I'd recite this verse as my intentional second thought. It became my go-to verse for driving, marking significant breakthroughs during that year. Although I started driving more frequently, lengthy drives or night-time ventures still unnerved me. It took years, but this verse, as my second thought, facilitated my healing journey with driving.

Seven years into my restoration journey, I finally felt ready physically to apply for a full-time position—a significant step forward. Throughout this phase, I continued to utilize intentional second thoughts, and that practice was pivotal in my progress. My recovery from all the physical symptoms was painstakingly gradual, leaving me uncertain about handling a full-time job's demands. I was unsure about the emotional toll, too.

I sought a position as a college pastor at the University of Iowa, serving with Parkview Church in Iowa City. During my candidating weekend—a series of meetings, interviews, activities, and public speaking—I constantly leaned on that comforting Bible verse from Isaiah. Driving through unfamiliar roads and neighborhoods at night, moments of doubt frequently crept in, questioning my capability. Fears surrounding potential panic attacks, heart irregularities, or sheer exhaustion raced through my mind, especially given the high stakes. Yet, every time, I reverted to that powerful verse:

"So do not fear, for I am with you; do not be dismayed, for I am your God. I will strengthen you and help you; I will uphold you with my righteous right hand."

Memorization and meditation support *The Power of the Second Thought.* God's reassuring words calmed and guided me, refocusing my thoughts. I felt a renewal of my spirit. God's presence and His promise of hope became my lifeline. That weekend, I not only managed to drive but was also offered the desired position. This was yet another testimony to the effectiveness of this habit. I felt like my struggles and challenges were so evident as I began the new position, yet God worked mightily. Our group of college students expanded from 20 to over 800, with people beginning a relationship with God every week. God moved in undeniable ways. Have you had seasons when you learned how to rely on God and cry out to Him in prayer? It's more about our availability than our ability. God's power is made perfect in our weaknesses. When we offer ourselves in service, God reveals his capabilities. He empowers us with new hope and perseverance. One of the ways God moves is to renew our minds. I realized in my healing journey that I would cultivate this habit of intentional second thoughts for the rest of my life.

Growth and Goals

It seems ironic that the Bible is my go-to source for intentional second thoughts because I didn't grow up reading the Bible. Suppose you are unfamiliar with scripture and the 66 books that make up the Bible. In that case, I want to encourage you to develop a hope habit that will serve as a storehouse of second thoughts for you to draw from in the years to come. I have listed a menu of verses in the Appendix. Those passages are great options as you choose your second thoughts. Spending time in God's Word will help build up your toolkit and provide your mind with new second thoughts. Memorization and meditation are powerful habits and nourish your soul. When you consider how to step into your purpose, it is wise to set goals. Goals are positive steps forward; they provide a framework and can ignite the flame in your soul. I set personal goals to learn the Bible. With new habits, you can set SMART goals. When I was trying to figure out my purpose, I began with an intentional goal of reading the entire Bible in a year. I believed that by spending that time with God and studying the life of Jesus, I would gain a clearer picture of the direction I needed in my life. It was a spiritual goal that would produce fruit in many other areas of life, including serving other people. God gives us the mind of Christ. The Bible contains God's thoughts and His ways.

When you set a goal, consider the SMART acronym: *Specific, Measurable, Attainable, Relevant,* and *Time-bound.* Here's what it looked like for me to set a SMART goal for reading Scripture:

Specific: What will I do? Read the Bible.

Measurable: What does success look like? Three chapters a day.

Attainable: How realistic is it? This only takes about 15 minutes.

Relevant: Why is it significant? I need a clearer sense of purpose and inspiration.

Time-bound: How long will it take? I will finish the Bible in a year.

SMART goals are essential because they protect us from being lazy, lacking direction, and setting goals that are too general and unhelpful. The goal you set is a tool to help you move forward in life. It involves reliance on God, not just human effort and resolutions. I believe the best goals are intentional and prayerful, not random. Goals can help maximize your potential and build momentum. Goals are catalytic and fuel growth.

When the year of Bible reading was completed, I realized that this was one of the most powerful goals I had ever set. It exceeded my expectations. It became a new habit for me every year and continues today in my walk with God. If you spend more time in the Bible, God will communicate more with you through His Word. The Bible really is a love letter drenched with hope. I have chosen to continue to practice that same goal every year of reading the entire Bible because it's so life-giving.

You will have your own SMART goals. Set aside some time today to think about your current situation and what you need to do to take the next steps with *The Power of the Second Thought*. Begin to identify what thoughts you will choose as your go-to during the day.

Clear and Compelling

Without goals, we tend to sit still and go nowhere. A lack of goals, direction, and purpose can hinder hope. Goals can move you past excuses and vague vision. It's a great way to find a clear and compelling purpose every day. Goals helped me grow spiritually and become familiar with God's Word. Now, I have a plan for the most difficult situations in my life. Memorizing the Bible was new; choosing verses and embracing *The Power of the Second Thought* was new. But through those four stages of development, I persevered. I want to encourage you to keep going because you're going to wonder, *Is this going to work? Can I really memorize this? Can I remember to use it during the day?*

It's time to take action and move past fears. Faith over fears. Action brings clarity. I encourage you right now to choose a specific second thought. It could be a Bible verse, a line from a song, or a poem. Your intentional second thought can be whatever you choose that is most helpful for you. Choose something that you will focus on for your second thought when negative first thoughts sneak into or even flood your mind. Select it now and write it down. Share it with a friend. Start to memorize it. Use this tool whenever you have a first thought that is taking you in the wrong direction in life, something that is untrue, destructive, selfish, mean, or full of despair. That's when you use your new tool. Tools shouldn't just collect dust or remain as intellectual options. They need to be used because they have a purpose. *The Power of the Second Thought* has a significant purpose and effectiveness in your life.

There will be a change in your thinking. This shift might happen gradually and infrequently at first. It might be tough to remember to replace your thoughts during the day, but soon, it'll become more natural. Over time, you'll transition from the first thought to the second thought rapidly and efficiently. You'll feel empowered and hopeful. Seeing the difference it makes in your life, attitude, and faith will be motivating.

The Power of the Second Thought will save you from unnecessary headaches and heartaches. It will shield you from worry and despair, protecting you from limiting beliefs, lies, and hope thieves. You will witness new victories, walking confidently in them and realizing that God is introducing access to hope that is greater than anything you have experienced before. Part of those victories will be in your mind, and God will develop and grow you. I want you to experience the fullness of this habit. God will provide everything you need to develop this new tool because hope is both relational and habitual.

I'm excited to journey with you this far. We have covered desiring hope and discovering a new tool and habit. In the final section of this book, I aim to guide you through a lifestyle of hope that leads to an unbreakable hope and deep security, allowing you to rest, risk, and redeem. God wants to transform both your inner life and the world around you. The final element is developing hope and experiencing the fullness of hope.

Cultivating Hope:

1. What are the four stages of developing a new habit?

2. What SMART goals do you want to have?

3. What is an intentional second thought you can start to focus on during the day?

Bible Study Questions:

1. What were some of Jesus' habits?

"But Jesus often withdrew to lonely places and prayed." (Luke 5:16)

2. How does God reward perseverance?

"Let us not become weary in doing good, for at the proper time we will reap a harvest if we do not give up." (Galatians 6:9)

3. What does it take to be a lifelong learner?

"Brothers and sisters, I do not consider myself yet to have taken hold of it. But one thing I do: Forgetting what is behind and straining toward what is ahead, I press on toward the goal to win the prize for which God has called me heavenward in Christ Jesus." (Philippians 3:13-14)

4. Why are these verses significant with habits and hope?

"Therefore, since we are surrounded by such a great cloud of witnesses, let us throw off everything that hinders and the sin that so easily entangles. And let us run with perseverance the race marked out for us, fixing our eyes on Jesus, the pioneer and perfecter of faith. For the joy set before him he endured the cross, scorning its shame, and sat down at the right hand of the throne of God." (Hebrews 12:1-2)

5. What is the Holy Spirit doing as we suffer?

"Not only so, but we also glory in our sufferings, because we know that suffering produces perseverance; perseverance, character; and character, hope. And hope does not put us to shame, because God's love has been poured out into our hearts through the Holy Spirit, who has been given to us." (Romans 5:3-5)

Scan this QR Code to dive deeper with Jesse and watch his video that provides additional stories, insights, and a prayer:

ELEMENT 3: DEVELOP

Inward Hope

Are you ready for a fresh vision and the fullness of hope? Sometimes, we only see a part of hope, or we categorize hope, or we give up on hope before realizing its fullness. It's important to remember that the fullness of hope is available to you every single day. This availability leads us into closeness with God because hope is relational.

In Luke 15, Jesus tells the story of a prodigal son. Usually, a child receives an inheritance after the parents die. But in this case, the son was selfish and eager. He wanted to gather his inheritance and run away from home to indulge in wild living. He pursued every pleasure and tasted everything this world had to offer, including time with prostitutes. As he indulged in wild living, he reached a low point when he ran out of money. He reached such a low place because pleasure ultimately cannot be found in anything created, and pleasure won't satisfy our souls. It wasn't just financial poverty; he also experienced poverty of the soul.

Welcome Home

He was longing for the food that the pigs were eating. In Jewish culture, pigs are seen as unclean. So, this was truly rock bottom. When you can't even acquire the food the pigs are eating, you are forced to reflect on your life and consider other options. Have you ever experienced a low point in life that became a springboard for a new direction and hope?

The Bible says he "came to his senses." He had a new thought, a second thought. His first thought was to gain distance from his father. The second thought is *I just want to be near Dad again.* He acted on his second thought. The change of thought and heart happen together. He realized, "Life was better with my father," and he returned home.

When we come to our senses, we come home to God—whether it's turning to God for the first time or returning to Him with all our hearts. As he arrived home, his father came running out. The father didn't bring shame and guilt; he brought love and grace. As the prodigal son came home, he was embraced and welcomed. There was a celebration, and grace was abundant. Have you been experiencing a longing to come home? Hope is relational, and God's grace surpasses our sin.

Hope and grace are connected. It is as if they are married in the sense that they're inseparable. Receiving God's grace paves the way to experience more of His hope. The fullness of grace introduces the fullness of hope.

The Power of the Second Thought is a habit that differs from typical notions of positive thinking. Sometimes, the phrase "positive thinking" is about merely feeling good. It's feeble and wishful, often not rooted in reality. For instance, if I claim I am about to run a four-minute mile, while many might cheer saying, "That's awesome!" and champion the spirit of positive thinking, realistically, I'm not going to run a mile that quickly. It's a fanciful thought. *The Power of the Second Thought,* on the other hand, is neither wishful nor baseless. It's grounded in truth and love. It presents a new, better, and hopeful direction and perspective. Why? Because it aligns with heaven. After all, if God is for you, who can be against you?

Rejecting and replacing thoughts involves faith, but it is not a blind faith. IT is a faith built on a solid relationship supported by historical evidence and facts. Right thinking guides you to the right feelings. However, the pursuit of mere positive thinking or positive feelings isn't the objective. Focusing solely on joy or peace will not get you there. The emphasis should be on a relationship with God, His presence, His Word, His character, and His marvelous deeds. When you are close to the God of all peace, the Prince of Peace, Jesus, joy is inherent in His presence. By concentrating on God's presence, you embrace a promise: draw near to God, and He will draw near to you. Right thinking leads to the right feelings naturally flowing from a renewed mind.

> *"Come near to God and he will come near to you. Wash your hands, you sinners, and purify your hearts, you double-minded." (James 4:8)*

> *"But seek first his kingdom and his righteousness, and all these things will be given to you as well" (Matthew 6:33). And, "Blessed are those who hunger and thirst for righteousness, for they will be filled." (Matthew 5:6)*

Light Over Darkness

It's important to recognize the many ways your new tool is effective. Jesus was very intentional with His thoughts. In Matthew chapter 4, verses 1-11, after His baptism coupled with confirmation and affirmation from His Heavenly Father that He was loved, Jesus found Himself in the wilderness. What followed His baptism? A challenging sojourn in the wilderness. Have you noticed how often major tests come right after victories? During this time, the devil appeared. Encountering the devil face-to-face is an intense experience. The devil tempted Jesus three times, and on each occasion, Jesus responded by quoting Scripture. Jesus was ready for the challenge and temptation. He had a second thought at the ready, anchored by the phrase, "It is written." Jesus wielded the Bible, the sword of the Spirit, as His defense. It is crucial to remain vigilant, especially after moments of celebration. Complacency or lowering your guard can provide openings for the enemy to undermine, steal, kill, and destroy your hope. Jesus is prepared for the mental and spiritual battle because He knows the Scripture. He is giving us a very practical example.

In the spiritual battle between good and evil, light and darkness, and God and the devil, we're equipped with the spiritual armor of God. Read Ephesians 6, verses 10-20, and note what God provides so that we can walk in the light. Among all the armor, there is one offensive weapon—the Word of God. Jesus had the Word ready. While He could have tackled temptation in various ways, He chose reliance on and the proclamation of God's Word while being tested to the core. Although Jesus was tempted as we are, He remained sinless. The initial thought or experience might be a temptation, but temptation itself is not sin. Jesus declared scripture, repelled temptation, and resisted the devil. Always remember: God consistently provides an escape route when faced with temptation. He remains faithful during our trials. Therefore, it's imperative to be prepared, as temptations arise daily. *The Power of the Second Thought* helps us overcome daily temptations. You can break free from sinful patterns, addictions, secret sins, and a double life!

"How can a young person stay on the path of purity? By living according to your word. I seek you with all my heart; do not let me stray from your commands. I have hidden your word in my heart that I might not sin against you." (Psalm 119:9-11)

Be prepared for temptation with scripture. You can say it out loud, memorize it, or read it; that approach will serve you best when faced with daily temptations. Many followers of Jesus don't pick up their "sword," lack a plan, or don't have an intentional second thought when tempted. Consequently, they feel confused. Some might entertain, harbor, or even welcome temptation because they aren't equipped. Jesus models this for us. Why did He choose Scripture? Because it's a choice available to us. It's an action we can take.

Your new tool and habit are applicable in every life situation. By now, the essence of hope and the value of intentional thinking should be clearer to you. It's crucial to understand that this is not merely cognitive. It is not just an intellectual exercise. Your thoughts permeate every facet of your life. Your mind and heart are intrinsically linked. When your mind is renewed, it steers your heart.

Your mind is also connected to your soul. For instance, when the prodigal son repents and "comes to his senses," he returns home. His attention, affection, and devotion return to his father. It's a picture of us returning to God. When Jesus declares Scripture, it's more than cognitive; it's profound. It relates to His purity, soul, and purpose. This isn't just confined to a mental or intellectual realm; your mind intertwines with both your heart and soul. I hope you grasp this as we explore the fullness of hope. We'll navigate through three sections: inward, outward, and upward. Throughout this journey, may God amplify and accelerate how we can develop hope and foster its growth in our lives.

Motivation and Transformation

I want to share a few stories in this section and more of God's word. As you read these stories, God continues to give fresh vision and new pictures of what hope can look like in your daily life.

Mark chapter 5 narrates the story of a demoniac—a man tormented by demons within him. Yes, it's true; demons are real. They are fallen angels who rebelled against God, and they can dominate a person's life. The spectrum ranges from temptation to oppression and, in extreme cases, to full possession. In this particular story, a legion of demons inhabited the man, causing immense torment. He harmed himself and was isolated. The town's people were engulfed in hopelessness, and the man likely felt utterly defeated. However, Jesus arrived and expelled those demons, heralding a triumph over darkness. His command was simple—"Leave." In Jesus' name, the demons complied. They entered a herd of pigs, which then rushed off a cliff.

One of the Bible's most disheartening verses describes how the townspeople responded by asking Jesus to leave their region. People choose their possessions over the Prince of Peace. Their concern for the pigs surpassed their compassion for the man. They didn't value that this man was now in his right mind, rescued, with a restoration that was so powerful. When Jesus commanded the demons to "leave," they obeyed, and the man who had started following Jesus asked, "Jesus, what would you have me do? Should I accompany you?"

Jesus responded, "No, share your testimony with your friends, family, and throughout the Decapolis, these ten cities."

Have you recently shared your story of how God has changed your life?

Find Your Voice

It's important to remember that when God acts in your life, don't remain silent or keep it hidden. Be ready to share your story. Perhaps God wants you to begin with your friends and family and in the places where you live, work, learn, and play. Just like the man in the previous story, there was an inward transformation; Jesus brought light and dispelled the darkness. God holds the power to chase away both the shadows and the fears of torment.

I resolved to share my story wherever and whenever God directed and nudged me, hoping more people would come to know Him and experience His hope. I recall the first time I was live on national television on ABC's Good Morning America. Being on the West Coast, it was incredibly early. The surreal feeling of waking up in complete darkness and preparing for that interview felt surreal. ABC had some technical difficulties as we waited to go on air—the audio just wouldn't work. With less than a minute before going live, our connection was still failing. The Bible says:

"Perfect love drives out fear." (John 4:18)

Anxiety welled up inside me. Will the interview even happen? What will I say? Could we fix the audio in time? Technical glitches are uniquely frustrating, but Jesus helps us overcome anxiety.

"Perfect love drives out fear."

Just seconds before the countdown ended, our audio link with New York City was restored, allowing the interview to proceed.

However, as soon as the interview began, the host veered off the expected script. The direction I anticipated for the interview wasn't where it was headed. Yet again, "Perfect love drives out fear." The love Jesus offers drives away demons, fear, anxiety, worry, or any trepidation you might feel in unfamiliar situations. Fear does not get the last word. It's always faith over fear. *The Power of the Second Thought* reinforces the message: God's perfect love drives away fear. Have you had moments when fear wanted to paralyze you, but you turned to God and redirected your thoughts?

Satisfied Souls

In the Bible (John chapter 3), we read about a man named Nicodemus. He is prestigious, holds a significant position and title, and is widely respected. Everyone looks up to him; he is moral and incredibly devout. Yet, despite his outward appearance, he harbors an emptiness within. The religious rules and rituals do not ignite his soul. While he maintains the facade, he lacks the living water that truly satisfies the soul. Meeting Jesus would be a controversial move for him at this time. It would likely be met with disapproval from his family, friends, and colleagues. Yet, driven by his desire for a greater hope and spiritual growth, he sneaks out at night to meet Jesus.

When Nicodemus approaches Jesus, he appears to seek knowledge. In response, Jesus recites what has become the most famous verse in the Bible, John 3:16:

"For God so loved the world that He gave His one and only Son, that whoever believes in Him shall not perish but have eternal life."

The core of this message is belief—a revolutionary concept for Nicodemus. He has spent his life striving to earn salvation, not realizing that all that's needed is to trust in Jesus. Jesus did it all. He accomplished our salvation, dying on the cross for our sins and conquering death in the grave. The gospel means good news and includes both Jesus' death and resurrection. Jesus is challenging Nicodemus' initial belief that he could earn heaven on merit alone. Jesus clarifies: salvation comes through faith in the Son of God, and He presents Nicodemus with a new, second thought that is true and good. Has Jesus ever changed your perspective and paradigm?

Over the last three years, we have launched hope campaigns and international television outreach programs. Countless viewers discreetly explore Jesus' teachings online. For many, embracing Jesus and getting baptized can lead to severe consequences like ostracism, imprisonment, or even physical harm. My personal journey echoed Nicodemus' hesitations. As my interest in Jesus grew, I grappled with the knowledge that many friends and family would disapprove of my curiosity and emerging faith. My first thought was fear-based, but my second thought was faith-based.

Currently, numerous countries have governments that attempt to suppress, block, or persecute people of faith. In many places, it's illegal to openly share your faith. People are imprisoned, assaulted, or even killed simply because they love Jesus. Despite His message of love and kindness, not everyone is prepared to accept the truth and allow others to experience the hope and goodness of God. Developing hope can have a high cost.

The Power of the Second Thought signifies a transformation in our minds, hearts, and souls: transitioning from unbelief to belief, from doubts to devotion, and from reluctance to restoration. A single Bible verse can alter both your day and your destiny. God's ability is limitless. Even if you're secretly reading about Jesus, feeling as though you're sneaking around to learn more, know that God sees and understands. He always offers an escape from temptation and introduces a second thought to transition you from fear to faith. Nicodemus was learning that inward hope is more valuable than external approval. What courageous decisions have you made recently?

No More Shame or Guilt

There's another individual in the Bible who discovered inward hope: his name is David. King David is often hailed as the greatest king in Israel's history. However, his imperfections are evident. The Bible paints a genuine portrait of real people, complete with their flaws. This is relevant and realistic because, as you dive into its pages, you realize that those who loved God were not so different from us today. They, too, had their share of shortcomings. David, for instance, had an affair with a woman and subsequently orchestrated the murder of her husband. Later in life, as a father, his passive nature led to turmoil within his household.

My intention isn't to list all of David's mistakes but to highlight that he didn't wallow in perpetual shame or guilt. In both Psalm 32 and Psalm 51, David bares his soul to God. God will never spurn someone who approaches Him with genuine contrition, humility, and a desire to return to His embrace. Psalm 32:5 underscores God's mercy and compassion, showing how He not only forgives our sins but also alleviates the burdens of guilt and shame that weigh us down.

"Then I acknowledged my sin to you and did not cover up my iniquity. I said, 'I will confess my transgressions to the Lord.' And you forgave the guilt of my sin." (Psalm 32:5)

God can renew you internally and infuse hope into situations that seem hopeless. The joy of the Lord entered David's life: the joy of the Holy Spirit, the joy of salvation. David didn't just experience this freedom; he also shared with others how they could attain the same freedom and forgiveness.

When you make bad decisions, do not let a spirit of shame and defeat define your life. There is grace in Jesus greater than our sins. Go to the Lord. He won't reject you.

"You will face many defeats in life, but never let yourself be defeated."
- Maya Angelou

"Restore to me the joy of your salvation and grant me a willing spirit, to sustain me. Then I will teach transgressors your ways, so that sinners will turn back to you." (Psalm 51:12-13)

David recognized that he didn't have to remain mired in shame and guilt; redemption was available. This profound forgiveness transformed him so deeply that he became known as a man after God's own heart. 1 Samuel 13:14 states:

"But now your kingdom will not endure; the Lord has sought out a man after his own heart and appointed him ruler of his people, because you have not kept the Lord's command."

After God set aside Saul, He made David their king. God's testimony about David is recorded in Acts 13:22:

"I have found David, son of Jesse, a man after my own heart; he will do everything I want him to do."

David's first thought was denial, but God led him to truth. David wanted a cover-up, but God brought honesty. David had shame, but God removed it. God has a second thought for us that brings restoration in every situation.

David remained faithful throughout his generation and led countless others to God. This demonstrates how new thoughts can change our path, creating a chain of spiritual momentum and helping sinful people learn to walk closely and humbly with God. Can you relate to David's story?

Roots and Fruit

A transformative second thought can pave a new path, acting as a gateway, initiating a wise shift in your mind. It opens the gates of heaven and unveils your life to God. This singular, inward reflection, this profound truth from heaven, becomes a conduit for transformation.

God's love is immeasurable, and He brings new thoughts to our mind that are saturated with hope. Understand that you can't guide others deeper than your own journey. God longs for personal and authentic connections with His people. Yet, many of us settle for a superficial relationship with Him, being content in thinking, *I'm on my way to heaven; why do I need to keep growing or have any sense of urgency?* But in reality, there's so much more— salvation includes eternal life, sin's forgiveness, and sanctification, where we grow to resemble Jesus more closely. Think of it as a fruit tree—robust roots yield bountiful fruit. Without healthy roots, the fruit will be lacking. Go deeper with God and allow Him to instill restoration, healing, forgiveness, and grace. Real breakthroughs manifest when God's truth permeates our deepest recesses, displacing the falsehoods and shame that once existed.

Howard Henderson said that you can impress from a distance, but you impact up close. Your most profound connections with others often stem not from your notable successes but from your raw honesty and vulnerabilities. God has used the adversities I've encountered to ignite a renewed purpose and passion. My connection and empathy for others is birthed from my experiences. Through my struggles, I've garnered insights into God's teachings and actions. I'm able to share what God has done for me, what He has taught me, and what has worked through Him so that others can journey through the valleys of the shadow of death rather than remain there. God will use your setbacks in life to both guide you into new comebacks and share with other people how to overcome what they are facing.

Grace and Truth

Jesus is a good shepherd who tends to His sheep. God's glory shines through our achievements and accomplishments and powerfully through the restoration He offers. God always enters with both truth and love. Jesus embodies both—he is filled with truth *and* overflowing with love. We need both. Love isn't merely a sentiment; it encompasses sacrifice, action, and commitment. Love and truth resemble two railroad tracks that consistently run parallel. God stands unwaveringly for both love and truth.

Transformation is most profound when we deeply internalize God's love and truth. In sharing your journey, being transparent in appropriate ways can showcase the hope God has instilled in you. If you find yourself trapped by hopelessness, invite God into those painful recesses. He has the power to transform even the direst circumstances into tremendous blessings, for He is the God of hope. Such is His inward work. Recall 2 Timothy 1:7:

"For the Spirit God gave us does not make us timid, but gives us power, love, and self-discipline."

Let this verse serve as an uplifting second thought to echo throughout your day. You'll find this thought indispensable in battling feelings of fear, worry, despair, shame, and guilt. It's a testament to the provision, power, perspective, and peace of God. Relying on mere performance is a fragile anchor for the soul, whereas God's grace offers the sturdy anchor we all need. Embrace this shift, allowing God to work profoundly within you. This internal process is crucial in nurturing hope and fostering inward hope.

When you consider the demoniac, Nicodemus, and David (an outcast, a religious leader, and a king), God demonstrates that He is able to bring inward hope to all people. Demon possession, empty religious systems, and egregious sin and cover-ups are not the story here. They are the starting point before God brings inward hope. Failure is not your leading story. Let God rewire your thinking and rewrite your destiny and legacy.

Cultivating Hope:

1. How does God help you win the battle in your mind?

2. What is your plan to handle temptation well?

3. What are some new victories in your faith that God can bring?

Bible Study Questions:

1. *What does it look like to have God as your top priority?*

"But seek first his kingdom and his righteousness, and all these things will be given to you as well. Therefore do not worry about tomorrow, for tomorrow will worry about itself. Each day has enough trouble of its own." (Matthew 6:33-34)

2. *How does God bless humility and increase hope?*

"Trust in the Lord with all your heart and lean not on your own understanding; in all your ways submit to him, and he will make your paths straight." (Proverbs 3:5-6)

3. *What is living water, and how do you receive it?*

"On the last and greatest day of the festival, Jesus stood and said in a loud voice, 'Let anyone who is thirsty come to me and drink. Whoever believes in me, as Scripture has said, rivers of living water will flow from within them.' By this, he meant the Spirit, whom those who believed in him were later to receive. Up to that time, the Spirit had not been given, since Jesus had not yet been glorified." (John 7:37-39)

4. *In what ways can you protect your hope?*

"Above all else, guard your heart, for everything you do flows from it. Keep your mouth free of perversity; keep corrupt talk far from your lips. Let your eyes look straight ahead; fix your gaze directly before you. Give careful thought to the paths for your feet and be steadfast in all your ways. Do not turn to the right or the left; keep your foot from evil." (Proverbs 4:23-27)

5. *What security does Jesus give you?*

"For I am convinced that neither death nor life, neither angels nor demons,[a] neither the present nor the future, nor any powers, neither height nor depth, nor anything else in all creation, will be able to separate us from the love of God that is in Christ Jesus our Lord." (Romans 8:38-39)

Scan this QR Code to dive deeper with Jesse and watch his video that provides additional stories, insights, and a prayer:

Outward Hope

An indestructible hope is both inward and outward. Let's expand our understanding of the outward development of hope. During my time in Zimbabwe, I was deeply moved by the life lessons I acquired from the people there. Materially and monetarily, they possessed far less than many Americans I knew. Yet, they were abundant in generosity, kindness, and hospitality. I learned that hospitality isn't about the size or cleanliness of your home or the balance in your bank account—it's about your character and the love in your heart.

The affection and warmth I felt in Africa, especially from the people of Zimbabwe, was instantaneous upon my arrival. The kids in Zimbabwe sang in the classrooms, even though they didn't have the financial or scholastic resources, they didn't have the job opportunities, they didn't have the teachers that we have, but they made the most of their opportunities and proceeded with gratitude and a spirit of victory. There was an overflow of hope in their hearts that was far greater than the endless obstacles and threats they faced. As a foreigner, this enduring memory of their unyielding hope deeply impacted me.

Outward hope and generosity remind me of the story of Zacchaeus in the Bible. As told in Luke chapter 19, he was wealthy but miserly, having accumulated his wealth through deceit and exploitation. Sadly, many in today's business world resemble Zacchaeus, achieving success through self-centered, dishonest, and materialistic pursuits. The love of money is the root of all types of bad decisions and evil. Zacchaeus' life was lacking close friendships and hope. He was a short man who climbed a tree so he could get a glimpse of Jesus. Getting one view of Jesus can change your life.

Engaging with Jesus can revolutionize not only individual lives but relationships as well. The quality of your relationships determines the quality of your life. Zacchaeus' interactions were strained because selfish people seldom build meaningful connections. Jesus sees selfish, crooked, and self-consumed people, yet he still loves them, pursues them, and wants to spend time with them. Jesus visited Zacchaeus' home. In this relational context, Zacchaeus' connection with Jesus transformed all his other relationships. The inward hope of God filled his mind and led to a new passion to give outward hope.

Indeed, a relationship with Jesus can redefine all your interactions. Being recipients of His forgiveness enables us to forgive others. Drawing hope from Him empowers us to inspire hope in others. Experiencing His generosity kindles our own sense of grace. Zacchaeus was a changed man and endeavored to right his wrongs. He became intent on restoring what he'd deceitfully amassed, even willing to part with half his wealth for the needy. He went from being someone who had a reputation for being stingy and selfish to being the most generous person in his community. How does that happen? Jesus has said it very clearly, "It's more blessed to give than to receive." This testimony not only rehabilitated his life but also positively impacted countless others. From being the most unscrupulous man, he emerged as an emblem of generosity and a beacon for justice. God brought an inward hope that led to an outward expression. Repentance included making it right. Zacchaeus' first inclination was selfishness, but Jesus flooded his heart and mind with new desires and hope. Zacchaeus' second season of life included second thoughts of compassion and kindness. He learned to value people more than possessions. He became a sacrificial giver who brought outward hope to his community. We can't stop with inward hope; outward hope is the next step forward.

The Purpose of Blessings

When God fills you with hope, it's connected to blessing many other people. God blesses you to be a blessing. This is the principle in scripture— you are blessed to bless others. Starting in Genesis 12, God profoundly blesses Abraham with land, seed, and blessing so that he will bless the nations. God blesses a nation to bless other nations. He blesses you to bless your neighbors. The blessings God brings you are attached to all the blessings God wants to bring through you. First, God works in you; then, he works through you. Don't stop when he blesses you, thinking that's the end of the story. That's just the beginning. The story starts with how Zacchaeus was able to bless so many others. The generosity Zacchaeus realized, experienced, discovered, and developed is the same generosity I witnessed in Zimbabwe, and it flows from hope. Are you experiencing a community that values and practices generosity together?

One Person at a Time

Regarding outward relationships, Ruth and Naomi are in-laws, as seen in the four chapters of the biblical Book of Ruth. Ruth and Naomi experienced tragedy. Life was great, and their marriages were joyous, but then their husbands died. They were left lonely and grieving without a backup plan. Naomi became bitter and contemplated leaving the community to return to her hometown. With the family connection weakened by tragedy, it seemed inevitable that Ruth and Naomi would part ways. However, Ruth made a choice rooted in loyalty. She proclaimed to Naomi:

> "Where you go, I will go; and where you stay, I will stay. Your people will be my people, and your God my God." (Ruth 1:16)

This declaration defined their relationship. When all external signs pointed to despair and isolation, God infused Ruth's heart with hope. This hope rejuvenated their bond, exemplifying God's love for us, which we often observe in relationships. Ruth's dedication to Naomi, even against Naomi's advice, epitomized selflessness and loyalty. One might initially think, *Okay, it looks like we won't live next to each other, and we won't share our lives anymore.* The initial thought might be tinged with sorrow, hinting that life will never regain its past celebrations. *The Power of the Second Thought* includes affection and devotion. Ruth decides: *I'm committed to this relationship. I will stay by your side and care for you.* Such a choice has been a beacon of inspiration for countless Generations and nations. Outward hope travels further than you realize. God multiplies impact and will always reward you for serving faithfully. There is no higher goal than faithfulness to God.

I remember when Laurie and I were in the process of adoption. We underwent six months of training and began with foster care. At that time, Elijah, who was four years old, visited our house. We had been spending increasing amounts of time with him, driving several hours just to share a meal or visit a park together. This particular visit marked his first overnight stay with us.

I have a habit of reading my Bible in my closet. While I was there, Elijah, curious as ever, explored our home. Eventually, he came into my room, noticed my Bible, and asked, "What's this?"

"It's God's word," I replied. "I enjoy reading it."

As he opened the Bible, I marveled at the fact that he could have turned to any page or section. Yet, he landed precisely on this passage:

"But Ruth replied, 'Don't urge me to leave you or to turn back from you. Where you go, I will go, and where you stay, I will stay. Your people will be my people, and your God my God. Where you die, I will die, and there

I will be buried. May the Lord deal with me, be it ever so severely, if even death separates you and me.'" (Ruth 1:16-17)

Pointing at it, he asked, "Read this."

As I read those verses aloud, I was profoundly moved by his choice. I felt like God was speaking to me. Whatever fears and doubts I carried around adoption dissipated. My new second thought was, *We are going to do this. God is with us. God, Laurie, and I all love Elijah.* Sometimes, new direction is confirmed by God and arises during our own reading, reflections, and intentionality. Other times, it feels divinely inspired, as if God is directly planting a word or revelation in our minds. Reading that passage to Elijah, I felt a resounding clarity that adopting him was our path forward, precisely what God intended. God clearly communicates to us, and His voice becomes our second thought. Second thoughts can be so much richer than first thoughts.

A Loyal Love

In the outward relationships that depict the hope of God, such as that between Ruth and Naomi, we witness God's unwavering hope, commitment, and love. Yet, there's another dimension to consider.

I briefly lived in Scotland, a land of brave, rugged individuals known for their pragmatism, wisdom, and candidness. Playing soccer there exposed me to a distinct locker room culture, unlike what I experienced in college. The atmosphere was one of fierce competition, exemplifying the "iron sharpens iron" adage. And when iron sharpens iron, sparks inevitably fly. This environment taught me about how to carry myself as a professional. Perhaps you've encountered settings, be it at work or in relationships, that posed similar challenges. They weren't necessarily always comfortable, but they were instrumental for personal growth. They presented a choice—step up or step down. You get focused, and you get the job done with God's help.

Sometimes, when we consider outward hope in loving other people, we only want a version of love that's easy, convenient, or feels like a Hallmark™ card. My experience in Scotland was neither easy nor familiar. It thoroughly tested my mettle. Life's hardships have a way of revealing our character. In such moments, genuine love demands that we rise above complaints and excuses. Ruth, too, could have lodged numerous complaints or crafted a myriad of excuses for not wholly loving or committing to Naomi. Their relationship stands as a reminder of the strength of hope. Outward hope is resilient and willing to go the extra mile. Love includes sacrifices. Are you sensing God wants you to make some specific sacrifice in this season?

I urge you to recognize that genuine hope is rugged. Embodying it means overcoming numerous excuses and complaints. Do not let these hinder your relationships, for the quality of life hinges on the quality of our relationships. Genuine hope loves, trusts, protects, and perseveres. If you're inclined to view hope as flimsy, feeble, or superficial, consider its inspiring determination, as demonstrated by Ruth and Naomi.

In our church, we are committed to living out this hope. "Grace Loves Auburn" is an event we hosted for the last twelve years. We open our doors and distribute items and resources that we've gathered over the year. It initially began as a baby shower giving out free resources and has since expanded to encompass everything a family might need. Everything is offered for free, and hundreds of families attend. People from diverse backgrounds, financial situations, ethnicities, and beliefs come together. The atmosphere is full with hope, felt throughout the church during the event.

According to research by Barna, Seattle holds the distinction of having the nation's second-highest de-churched rate. Many individuals have faced negative experiences with churches. But when they enter our church and encounter genuine warmth, authenticity, and kindness—not to mention finding essentials for their family's needs that week or month—there's an undeniable sense of celebration and connection. For those who've been wounded in relationships, positive interactions can serve as God's means for healing. "Grace Loves Auburn" is more than just the items we give away; it's about fostering relationships and, most importantly, igniting hope. God is truly good. Numerous attendees have rekindled their faith, and their perceptions of God reshaped through conversations, love, and enjoyable relationships. When you make the effort to love others genuinely, the resulting healing can be transformative. Do you have any favorite events or gatherings where you sense God's presence and hope?

Hope, indeed, has the power to heal deeply. We've also collaborated with other churches on an initiative named the "Compassion Clinic." Here, physical therapists, dentists, physicians, and chiropractors offer their services for free. Much like "Grace Loves Auburn," the resulting hope and healing are profound.

It's great to read hope stories in the Bible, but God wants hope to fill our homes, communities, churches, and cities. I share these experiences to encourage you. God moves most profoundly when we take risks in building relationships. These endeavors can indeed be risky. Bringing hope might directly push you out of your comfort zone. Yet, it's in these moments that God accomplishes His greatest work. I urge you to keep forging these bonds. Take risks in serving, listening, and opening your heart and home. Embrace the unfamiliar, and God will guide you in authentically loving your neighbor, including friendships with people from all cultures and nations.

Love Your Neighbors

Loving your neighbor might sound like a straightforward concept. Yet, many find it easier to discuss than to practice. Pastors might find it more comfortable to preach about it than to live it. Bible study groups may prefer to dissect the idea rather than embody it. When questioned:

"'Teacher, which is the greatest commandment in the Law?' Jesus replied: 'Love the Lord your God with all your heart and with all your soul and with all your mind.' This is the first and greatest commandment. And the second is like it: 'Love your neighbor as yourself.' All the Law and the Prophets hang on these two commandments." (Matthew 22:36-40)

So, what's the greatest commandment? How does one encapsulate scripture? Jesus articulated that first, we must love God with every facet of our being. Then, we should love our neighbors as we love ourselves.

Consider this: Who are the people in your family? Who lives next to you? Do you recognize and know the people on your block? Are you familiar with their names and their stories? Do you genuinely care for them? Think about your colleagues or classmates because anyone in need who you can assist qualifies as your neighbor. Making the act of loving your neighbor a habitual thought can profoundly transform your relationships. Waking up each day with the question, "Who can I bless today?" leads to a new focus on outward hope. Embracing this perspective and asking, "Who is a neighbor I can show love to today?" allows God to work mightily through you. I challenge you to live this approach daily.

When the pandemic began, a man I know, employed full-time at a public school and a father to two young children, faced a challenging situation. Given the demands of the pandemic, his initial reaction could easily have been, "There's nothing I can do; I lack time, energy, and resources." However, the "love your neighbor" anthem resonates deeply within him. He collaborated with various organizations and developed teams to support his community, distributing over 15 million pounds of food.

When you start with the thought, *Love your neighbor*, you don't know where the journey will take you. But take that step in faith, allowing God to chart the course and write the script. *The Power of the Second Thought* is a habit that is inherently action-oriented. Faith devoid of deeds is dead, and no one wants a dead faith. It originates internally; it becomes an external hope, resulting in faith that takes action.

Intentionally Bless

If you want to gain an instant sense of purpose and provide hope to people, begin each morning with a commitment to being generous. Ask yourself, *Who can I bless today?* God blesses us so we can, in turn, bless others. In the book of Genesis, we learn that God blessed Abraham with the intent that he would be a blessing to all nations. Each of us has the daily opportunity to live a life of generosity rather than hoarding our blessings. By blessing others, you lay a foundation for hope and become a beacon of hope in your community. If the concept of blessing others seems too broad or nebulous, let's go deeper with a helpful acronym, **B.L.E.S.S.** It translates into five specific action points, reinforcing the idea that love is more about actions than feelings:

- **B**egin With Prayer.
- **L**isten Well.
- **E**at Together.
- **S**erve One Another.
- **S**hare Your Story.

Begin With Prayer: Prayer is simply communication with God. As you listen to God and bring your requests to Him, know that prayer is powerful. God answers prayer. When you intercede for others and their needs, you act in love. Prayer is humbling, kind, caring, wise, and effective.

Make a list of your friends, relatives, acquaintances, neighbors, and co-workers. Add them to your prayer list and intentionally lift them up to heaven through prayer. Perhaps you're reading this chapter and haven't yet come to believe in God. Maybe prayer is a completely new concept to you. Embarking on this journey will be an adventure. It might take some time and effort before you begin to feel at ease.

Prayer isn't just a formula, nor is it a waste of time. I remember the very first time I spoke to God in prayer. I was in college. It marked a significant shift in my life because I had come to understand that I wasn't entirely self-sufficient. There exists a greater source of love, hope, forgiveness, and kindness. When I reached out to Him, God began filling me with these virtues. I learned to pray for others, and through those prayers, God transformed many situations and lives.

There's no limit to what God can accomplish in you and through you.

Listen Well: Blessing others involves listening with your ears, your heart, and your mind. It goes beyond merely hearing the words they say. It's more than just formulating your reply while they're speaking. And it isn't always about finding a solution. True listening means engaging emotionally and striving for understanding.

Ask questions. Engage the other person and seek to understand their perspective. This can be especially challenging for extroverts. The Bible says:

"My dear brothers and sisters, take note of this: Everyone should be quick to listen, slow to speak and slow to become angry." (James 1:19)

Such advice is a solid foundation for any healthy relationship. Just imagine the impact if we all began from this point. Consider the love and healing we might foster within our families, communities, and even our nation.

It's natural for me to speak first rather than listen. This tendency can be counterproductive, especially in situations I want to quickly solve and provide a remedy. It's essential to observe the tone, body language, and facial expressions of the speaker. For instance, when someone says they are "fine," it might not always be the full story. What are they truly trying to convey? Listen attentively. When you genuinely listen to people, they will feel your value and love for them.

Eat Together: In many cultures, sharing a meal in a home conveys a profound sense of acceptance and family. Across all cultures, dining together offers a chance to strengthen connections and friendships. Food encourages us to take a moment to relax. It's a pleasure. It fosters an environment ripe for genuine conversation. Food addresses a daily need and provides nourishment. I mean, who doesn't enjoy good food?

Relationships come with risks. It requires courage to connect, to show vulnerability, and to be open about one's beliefs, ideas, and dreams. Many of these deep connections happen over shared meals. Spend time with people. Treat them to a meal. Invite guests into your home. It could be for coffee, tea, smoothies, or dessert. Deliver a meal to someone who's going through a tough time or feels isolated. Offer a meal to a homeless individual. Host a block party and supply the BBQ and ice cream for everyone. Get creative and cherish the moments spent together.

Serve One Another: What needs do the people around you have? Are they physical, financial, emotional, spiritual, or relational? How can you assist them? Ask God to reveal to you the needs you can address. Perhaps someone needs a ride because they have no means of transportation. Maybe another person requires help with yard work as they can't manage it themselves. It could be that a word of encouragement, accompanied by a surprise gift card, would brighten someone's day. Or perhaps all they need is friendship, and an invitation to a gathering would suffice. You possess resources capable of making significant impacts in both big and small ways. Our church recently sponsored over 200 children in Cambodia due to their unmet basic needs. And don't forget your talents—both your words and actions can accomplish wonders. How do you enjoy serving others? Who are you naturally drawn to?

Who captures your attention and affection? Sometimes, your own emotions guide your actions. Serving others brings fulfillment to everyone involved.

Share Your Story: Open up about your experiences, struggles, and lessons learned. Talk about your faith journey. Spread the hope you hold. Share a Bible verse that's meaningful to you. Recommend a book you love. Direct someone to a resourceful website. Quote words of wisdom. Discuss the lessons God has been teaching you. Share from the depths of your heart.

Each morning, consider how you can make a difference in someone's day. Such an outlook can be transformative because we find our true purpose in this mindset. Today isn't just about self-focus; it's about the community around us. Instead of "What's best for me?" we can shift to "What's best for us?"

The Bible tells us that Jesus did not come to be served but to serve.

"When the ten heard about this, they became indignant with James and John. Jesus called them together and said, 'You know that those who are regarded as rulers of the Gentiles lord it over them, and their high officials exercise authority over them. Not so with you. Instead, whoever wants to become great among you must be your servant, and whoever wants to be first must be slave of all. For even the Son of Man did not come to be served, but to serve, and to give his life as a ransom for many.'" (Mark 10:41-45)

To be more Christ-like is to bless others. Reflect on the ways God has blessed you, and look for opportunities to pass those blessings on. God will use you in unexpected and wonderful ways throughout each day. This journey will bring about profound change, not only in those you help but in you as well. And always remember this truth: you can never out-give God. As you extend blessings to others, God showers you with even greater blessings.

Radical Compassion

When you say "yes" to God, blessings flow to others through you. The script God might pen and the wonders He might bring are beyond our comprehension.

"Now to him who is able to do immeasurably more than all we ask or imagine, according to his power that is at work within us" (Ephesians 3:20)

It all begins with the fundamental thought of loving one's neighbor and recognizing the immense possibilities springing from that outward hope.

In John chapter 4, we encounter a woman at a well who has been married multiple times. Relationships haven't filled her void; no individual can quench the soul's deepest thirst. Her daily trips to the well offer no contentment, and her religion seems lifeless. She's entangled in misconceptions yet meets Jesus and experiences His unparalleled compassion and hope.

Read the Gospels—Matthew, Mark, Luke, and John. Observe Jesus, who consistently infuses hope, often defying societal norms. His actions are revolutionary. Despite being a Jewish man, He interacts with a Samaritan woman, a blend of Jewish and Gentile heritage, often scorned by full-blooded Jews. Remarkably, Jesus, a sinless Rabbi, chooses to converse with her, countering the cultural norm that relegated women to a secondary status. Jesus' purity in connecting with a woman notorious for her transgressions is an expression of His limitless love—He'd forsake the ninety-nine to save the one. Such love can be perplexing, even unsettling, to some religious minds.

Many religious individuals resist unrestrained hope, balk at radical compassion, and cringe at breaking societal boundaries. They prefer maintaining external veneers rather than embracing God's true intent. To emulate God's love, we need to perceive others as He does. Our hearts should resonate with His, breaking when His breaks. Drawing close to the Samaritan woman, Jesus speaks of the "living water" for her spirit. For once, she perceives the Messiah, and her hope is rejuvenated. Once reclusive and burdened with guilt and shame, this woman finds value in Jesus' eyes. Her identity isn't tied to her past or actions; Jesus uplifts and empowers her. Realizing Jesus as the Messiah, the notion of "living water" becomes her guiding principle.

"Living water" fills her mind, heart, and soul. She goes around town, shares her revelation with her community, and brings many to Jesus. Intriguingly, at this juncture, Jesus's followers are more perturbed about Him conversing with this woman, urging Him, "Jesus, eat some food."

In John 4:34, Jesus responds:

"My food is to do the will of him who sent me and to finish his work."

The disciples struggle to grasp the depth of compassion and hope. They miss this expansive nature of hope. Yet, this woman, without seminary training, lacking extensive Bible studies, and without a lengthy history of walking with Jesus, instantly comprehends the essence of hope. It's an inward reception and an outward sharing. Having freely received this hope, she freely gives it. Consequently, she becomes a beacon in her community, guiding many to discover Jesus, the source of living water and hope.

Start with Family

Never give up on people, regardless of their age or life situation. My grandfather, for instance, came to know Jesus in his 70s. Following that transformation, his health declined, and he faced multiple issues, such as low blood cell counts, shingles, and strokes. With every hospital visit, his physical and cognitive abilities diminished. Despite living out of state, I would often visit him. Our bond deepened over time, and he became the sole family member with whom I shared the same faith. Our weekly conversations and prayers were the highlight of my days. My grandpa had multiple bookmarks in his Bible, and when asked about it, he'd reply, "I just can't get enough. I'm really growing in my relationship with God."

I'd respond, "You're spending so much time with God."

"I just want to know God before I see Him and be with Him." His faith grew, even as strokes took away his speech.

During those trips, I'd also spend nights with my grandmother. She had long resisted embracing faith and God's love. But watching the transformation in my grandpa, her heart began to soften. We delved deeper into discussions about faith during my stays.

One evening, after her exercise routines and a Dove chocolate bar (which seemed to inject her with energy), we talked about a relationship with God until 2:00 in the morning. While she had some religious background, she had never chosen to follow Jesus. That night, she did. She decided to embrace the gift of eternal life, the forgiveness of sins, and to make peace with God. I vividly recall that night; as we prepared to sleep, she joyfully shouted, "Jesse, you can sleep well tonight because I believe what you believe." After placing her trust in Jesus, my grandma's life overflowed with joy.

I visited Grandpa in the hospital the following day. Though he couldn't speak, I relayed the story to him. Tears of joy streamed down his face upon hearing that his wife would one day join him in heaven. He embraced this heartwarming news before he passed on to be with Jesus. As for my grandma, she's nearing 100 now and is still with us.

I share this to emphasize that we can never truly predict who will open their heart to God's love. Many might have dismissed the woman at the well, just as those who knew my grandma for decades might have believed she'd never turn to God. Yet, we must never underestimate the transformative power of God's love. When we persevere in our faith, develop a growing outward hope, and become instruments of God's message of hope, there's no limit to what God can do.

Hospitality and Hope

When God's hope fills your heart, your home becomes an open space. This hope nudges open the front doors of our homes. When we invite our neighbors in, we often underestimate what can transpire within our four walls. There can be shared meals, hearty laughter, and a sense of relaxation. Your home transforms into a sanctuary of hope. Do you envision your living space in this light? Whether it's an apartment, condominium, or house, it can transform into a beacon of hope. In America, especially post-pandemic, we need to re-embrace the art of hospitality. For hope truly thrives at home. By welcoming others, we don't just narrate tales of hope; we let them experience it.

Our house serves as a hub in our neighborhood for games, fun, and friendships. With four kids constantly inviting their friends over, there's a perpetual flow of guests. The backyard has two soccer goals. While my wife would like a lush green lawn, it currently displays a patchwork of grass and dirt—a reflection of the countless soccer games played there. We've prioritized relationships over aesthetics. Our backyard, for now, remains a favored gathering spot. Add to that a trampoline and a basketball hoop in the front yard. The living room even features a Pop-A-Shot game. And yes, things occasionally break when guests come, but the trade-off is invaluable.

I know a couple who have welcomed over 100 foster kids into their home. The county often reaches out to them during dire circumstances. Many of these children have faced traumatic experiences, from prenatal drug and alcohol exposure to physical abuse. Yet, this couple provides them with a haven, perpetuating the narrative of hope. God's hope, once instilled in us, cannot be contained. It overflows, extending from us to others, driven by love and compassion. As you open up your heart, you naturally open your home. When you turn the key to your front door, you're also unlocking the vast potential of hope. Take relational risks grounded in humility, and leave the outcomes in God's hands.

This chapter includes a wide range of Bible and real-life stories. What stories of outward hope are you celebrating? God works in you, through you, and beyond you.

Cultivating Hope:

1. Why is loyal love so rare and powerful?

2. How does Jesus motivate you to be generous?

3. Who can you BLESS this week?

Bible Study Questions:

1. How has God called you to give hope to people?

"There will always be poor people in the land. Therefore I command you to be openhanded toward your fellow Israelites who are poor and needy in your land." (Deuteronomy 15:11)

2. What are some ways you can bless people this week?

"For I was hungry and you gave me something to eat, I was thirsty and you gave me something to drink, I was a stranger and you invited me in, I needed clothes and you clothed me, I was sick and you looked after me, I was in prison and you came to visit me."

"Then the righteous will answer him, 'Lord, when did we see you hungry and feed you, or thirsty and give you something to drink? When did we

---

see you a stranger and invite you in, or needing clothes and clothe you? When did we see you sick or in prison and go to visit you?'"

"The King will reply, 'Truly I tell you, whatever you did for one of the least of these brothers and sisters of mine, you did for me.'" (Matthew 25:35-40)

3. What is taught about hope and generosity in these verses?

"Remember this: Whoever sows sparingly will also reap sparingly, and whoever sows generously will also reap generously. Each of you should give what you have decided in your heart to give, not reluctantly or under compulsion, for God loves a cheerful giver. And God is able to bless you abundantly, so that in all things at all times, having all that you need, you will abound in every good work. As it is written: 'He has scattered abroad his gifts to the poor; his righteousness endures forever.' Now he who supplies seed to the sower and bread for food will also supply and increase your store of seed and will enlarge the harvest of your righteousness. You will be enriched in every way so that you can be generous on every occasion, and through us your generosity will result in thanksgiving to God." (2 Corinthians 9:6-11)

4. What are the purposes of God's blessings?

"May God be gracious to us and bless us and make his face shine on us— so that your ways may be known on earth, your salvation among all nations. May the peoples praise you, God; may all the peoples praise you. May the nations be glad and sing for joy, for you rule the peoples with equity and guide the nations of the earth. May the peoples praise you, God; may all the peoples praise you. The land yields its harvest; God, our God, blesses us. May God bless us still, so that all the ends of the earth will fear him." (Psalm 67)

5. How can your words bring hope to people daily?

"But in your hearts revere Christ as Lord. Always be prepared to give an answer to everyone who asks you to give the reason for the hope that you have. But do this with gentleness and respect, keeping a clear conscience, so that those who speak maliciously against your good behavior in Christ may be ashamed of their slander." (1 Peter 3:15-16)

Scan this QR Code to dive deeper with Jesse and watch his video that provides additional stories, insights, and a prayer:

Upward Hope

The fullness of hope includes an inward hope, an outward hope, and an upward hope. Anyone can strike up a song of hope, and when directed towards God, it elevates our spirits. An inspiring account from the Bible in Acts chapter 16 resonates deeply with me. It recounts the story of a jailer overseeing the Apostle Paul and Silas, who were incarcerated. Despite it being midnight and despite their unjust imprisonment, Paul and Silas began to sing a song of hope. Though one might expect to be punished for grave offenses, Paul and Silas were innocent. Yet, they opted to sing, highlighting that hope is always a choice.

Their act of faith didn't go unnoticed. Other inmates and the jailer observed their unwavering faith. As they sang, suddenly, an earthquake shook the prison. Chains were broken, and God delivered them in a spectacular manner. The jailer, fearing repercussions from the apparent escape of the prisoners, contemplated suicide.

The tragic reality is many today, feeling trapped in despair, see ending their life as the only way out. Suicide, however, offers no solace. It's a permanent resolution to temporary struggles. Having lost two family members to suicide, I cannot emphasize enough the gift and importance of life. Witnessing the jailer's desperate state, Paul, filled with hope and compassion, assured him of their presence. He then introduced him to the boundless love of God. That very night, the jailer and his entire household turned to Jesus and were baptized. The aftermath? A church was established in that city, the Gospel spread across Europe, and hope became contagious.

What sparked this widespread revival? A simple act of looking upward in hope. This ignited a chain reaction—preventing a suicide, saving a family, transforming a community, influencing a nation, and eventually touching the world.

A Harvard study on human flourishing indicates that active participation in one's faith leads to heightened levels of happiness, purpose, forgiveness, and generosity. Additionally, it correlates with reduced rates of depression, illicit drug use, and sexually transmitted diseases. The Ivy League research confirms how important it is to connect with God. This upward hope has a tangible positive influence on our mood, interpersonal relationships, sense of purpose, and overall physical and mental well-being. The blessings God bestows upon you are divinely connected to the blessings you will extend to others in your day-to-day environments.

Local and Global

Hope is not stationary; it travels. Acts chapter 8, verses 26-40, introduces us to an Ethiopian whom Philip encounters. This Ethiopian is attempting to decipher Scripture, finding it perplexing. For those unfamiliar with the Bible from childhood, it can indeed be daunting. With Philip's guidance, he comprehends the scriptures' message about Jesus. The Ethiopian embraces this knowledge, places his faith in Jesus, gets baptized, and subsequently, the gospel finds its way to Africa. This upward gaze of hope, beginning with a single individual, has the potential to influence an entire continent. So, if you ever feel disheartened about the state of your community or nation, remember that hope often originates from a single source.

It commences with you, extends outwards, and then proliferates. Reflect upon the jailer's experience and how hope's influence radiated and multiplied.

In today's era, with the aid of technology, the potential acceleration of hope has taken on unprecedented speed. Through platforms like social media, you can impart hope to hundreds, even thousands. The digital realm has exponentially expanded our capacity to communicate hope. A surge in online searches reflects an unprecedented hunger for hope. Historically unparalleled numbers indicate people's fervent longing for God, hope, and peace. A palpable thirst resonates within their souls.

We have been involved in digital campaigns, which we often call "hope campaigns" or "hope initiatives." Through a typical outreach, we have usually witnessed 10,000, 20,000, or even 30,000 individuals begin a relationship with God. One particular outreach coincided with the World Cup. It's worth noting that my soccer career, unfortunately, came to an end in my 20s. Despite once believing I'd play for much longer (considering that goalkeepers sometimes play into their 40s), my dreams were cut short. For years, I grappled with the grief and sense of loss because I couldn't realize my aspirations in soccer.

During the World Cup, however, I found an opportunity to share hope. I narrated my journey and explained the truth about heaven. The audience online watched the videos and learned more about both heaven and the hope of God for today. The World Cup brings nations together, and similarly, heaven will be home to people from every language, tribe, and nation. While soccer is central to the World Cup, Jesus is the focal point in heaven. Heaven isn't just an abstract idea; it's a tangible, eternal reality. Through that message, over 480,000 people chose to place their faith in Jesus. When you describe real hope, it inspires individuals to redirect their gaze upwards. It draws them out of despair and fosters a connection with God.

Unexpected Hope

When contemplating upward hope, reflect on Joseph and Mary. In Matthew chapter 1, verses 18-25, their initial reaction was:

"Let's have a discreet divorce."

Why? Because how does one explain a pregnancy without intimacy? How does one convey the idea of a virgin birth or an immaculate conception? It's a narrative that's almost impossible to share in a manner that others would readily accept and believe. They anticipated societal ostracization, judgment, and maltreatment. Their primary instinct was a quiet divorce. Yet, God introduced a new solution and explanation, and they chose to trust in Him. Their first thought was divorce, but their second thought was from God. If your second thought aligns with God, you can navigate any detour or difficulty. As the narrative unfolds, Mary proclaims her role as God's servant.

A profound piece of advice emerges from the Wedding at Cana, where Jesus converted ceremonial water into wine:

"On the third day, a wedding took place at Cana in Galilee. Jesus' mother was there, and Jesus and his disciples had also been invited to the wedding. When the wine ran out, Jesus' mother informed Him, 'They have no more wine.'

'Woman, why do you involve me?' Jesus replied. 'My hour has not yet come.'

His mother instructed the servants, 'Do whatever he tells you.'

Nearby, six stone water jars, typically used by the Jews for ceremonial washing and capable of holding twenty to thirty gallons each, stood filled. Jesus directed the servants, 'Fill the jars with water.' They did so, filling them to the brim.

Then He said, 'Now draw some out and take it to the master of the banquet.'

Upon doing so, the master of the banquet tasted the water, now transformed into wine. Unaware of its origin, though the servants who fetched the water were privy to it, he pulled the bridegroom aside, remarking, 'Usually, one serves the choice wine first, followed by the cheaper wine once guests have had their fill. But you have reserved the best for last.'

This miraculous act in Cana of Galilee was among the initial signs Jesus performed, showcasing His divine glory, leading His disciples to believe in Him. Following this, Jesus, accompanied by His mother, brothers, and disciples, traveled to Capernaum, where they spent a few days." (John 2:1-12)

Weddings in that era spanned several days. Running out of wine before the festivities concluded would have been a significant embarrassment. In addressing those whom Jesus instructed to procure the ceremonial jars:

"His mother said to the servants, 'Do whatever he tells you.'" (John 2:5)

This guidance from Mary is perhaps some of the most profound advice we could ever receive in our journey with Jesus. Mary's proclamation stems from her personal experience. She and Joseph were thinking about divorce before they chose a new path forward as God guided them with a redemptive second thought that included His wisdom. Mary's anthem and advice to others at the wedding became the message: "Do whatever Jesus says."

Jesus's choice to utilize ceremonial jars is notable. In many cultures, wine symbolizes joy. Through this act, Jesus conveyed that a new, superior joy was accessible and not found in religious rituals. Instead, it was rooted in a relationship with the world's Savior. While Jesus was addressing a physical need at the wedding, the deeper significance lay in His revelation of His identity through this miracle, pointing people towards that profound joy and directing their focus upwards.

When you think about that shift, sometimes the second thought gives us a clear view of God, deepening our faith. At times, our trust in God may waver. However, when you utilize *The Power of the Second Thought*, there can be a realignment, a redirecting to trust God. The faith journey of Joseph and Mary exemplifies this truth. Their lives, filled with blessings, were profoundly impacted by their unwavering belief in God. Have you ever known the right solution, but it was very difficult to explain or convince others?

Receiving Hope

I know a couple who run a ministry addressing human trafficking. Many shy away from assisting because of the risks and potential high costs. Some prefer to play it safe. Yet, this couple commits to doing whatever Jesus calls them to, courageously aiding in the restoration process for those ensnared in human trafficking. These victims experience God's love and hope. They are welcomed into our church, where they grow in faith, hope, and love. Reflect on the healing God offers all of us and the hope of a new start that He provides. God can transform situations in our lives characterized by disbelief, doubt, and the worst of human behaviors, bringing forth beauty from ashes and joy from despair, as the prophet Isaiah describes. This embodies the essence of upward hope, a demonstration of God's grace.

John chapter 11 provides insights into understanding upward hope. Mary and Martha were initially disappointed with Jesus due to His timing. When their brother Lazarus fell ill, their immediate reaction was rooted in thoughts like, *God missed it. God delayed. God doesn't care.* They had hoped Jesus would come and heal him, but Lazarus passed away. As they grieved, Jesus made His appearance. His delay was intentional, reflecting a grander plan they couldn't perceive. The shortest verse in the Bible:

"Jesus wept." (John 11:35)

This is a poignant reminder of God's empathy. It underscores that God genuinely cares, deeply empathizing with our pain and anguish. Jesus is no stranger to sorrow.

Yet, within that same narrative, at Lazarus's funeral, Jesus proclaimed:

"Jesus said to her, 'I am the resurrection and the life. The one who believes in me will live, even though they die; and whoever lives by believing in me will never die. Do you believe this?'" (John 11:25-26)

At that moment, grief and hope converged, with hope prevailing over the sorrow. While grieving is a necessary, spiritual, and crucial process, we possess a hope in Jesus that towers above our grief.

We look upward. He is the resurrection and the life. He didn't merely *say* he's the resurrection and the life; he embodied it. It wasn't just rhetoric; it was a tangible reality. And Jesus always supports his declarations with actions. He manifested His dominion over death when he loudly commanded:

"Lazarus, come out!" (John 11:43)

And Lazarus emerged.

Mary and Martha realized that God always remains sovereign. God has the definitive voice. Our trust in Him remains intact. Jesus, being the resurrection and the life, manifested His power over death once more when, on the third day, He rose from the grave.

After Lazarus removed his burial clothes, he had a powerful testimony to share, guiding others toward faith. The profound impact of changing one's perspective became clear when Mary and Martha realized the depth of Jesus' trustworthiness. They recognized the perfection of Jesus' timing, His supremacy over death, and that He always has the last word. They realized Jesus' immense love and His deep empathy towards our sufferings. It took time, but these revelations bolstered the faith of Mary, Martha, Lazarus, and their entire community. Hope can indeed be cultivated and nurtured. Hope always looks upward.

Looking Up to God

One of the beautiful ministries I have the privilege to witness at our church is "Drive Thru Prayer." We collaborate with other churches in this endeavor because hope accelerates and expands through collaboration. While we might go faster alone, we go further together. Every Friday night, from 5:00 to 7:00, at the edge of our campus on the busiest street in our town, we have teams of people holding up signs offering prayer. They read, *"Do you need prayer?"* and *"Drive-thru prayer."* People drive their cars into the parking lot to receive prayer. Some are in tears, sharing their stories of pain and loss. Others wonder if they need to pay money, to which we respond, "No, this is free." People come to know Jesus and experience healing through this outreach.

One man, after an argument with his wife, was on his way to a casino, thinking it would be his solution. But upon seeing our signs, he pulled in. After explaining the recent conflict with his wife and receiving prayer, he decided against the casino. Instead, he chose to return to his wife, apologize, reconcile, and work on restoring their marriage. This demonstrates how looking upward or seeking the vertical connection with God can lead to positive horizontal outcomes in our relationships and actions. When you have a clear view of Jesus, you tap into a well of hope that never runs dry. God's reservoir of hope is boundless.

America desperately needs this upward hope. While our national motto is "In God We Trust," its significance has faded in our collective consciousness. Even if this motto is printed on our currency, it doesn't necessarily mean we're living out its message. The message we need to hear is present on every dollar bill, reminding us to shift from unbelief to belief. *The Power of the Second Thought* recalibrates our souls with upward hope.

"What gives me the most hope every day is God's grace; knowing that His grace is going to give me the strength for whatever I face, knowing that nothing is a surprise to God."
- Rick Warren

Take some time to reflect and meditate on these truths about the God of hope who can transform us with His presence. God's greatest gift is His presence.

In Him, you will find hope. In Him, you will find love. In Him, you will experience peace. In Him, you have forgiveness of sins. Your identity is secure in Him, providing an anchor for your soul. If you've never made the decision, I encourage you to put your trust in Jesus and embrace His hope now. Hope is a joyful and confident trust in someone or something. God's hope is inward, outward, and upward. Ultimately, God's hope is indestructible. Choosing hope, just like deciding where to drop your anchor, is a choice.

Indestructible Hope

Hope is available. It's relational. It's habitual in its cultivation. And most importantly, hope is indestructible. I want to highlight this truth about hope, understanding that some might be skeptical. Perhaps you're a bit cynical about the idea of hope. Maybe you've experienced significant loss, and the very notion of an indestructible hope seems far-fetched, even too good to be true. Indeed, God's hope might seem that way. If it feels too good to be true, then you're beginning to grasp its essence. This hope is indestructible precisely because God is. God's promises, heaven, His kingdom, and His love—all are unbreakable. While people can attempt to resist, deny, or even criticize God's love and hope, they cannot quench it. Consider Jesus: one might choose not to believe in the resurrection, but disbelief doesn't negate its reality.

If everyone had told Jesus that He couldn't overcome death, their disbelief wouldn't have altered the outcome. The resurrection remains an unstoppable event, showcasing that God's hope is indestructible. If our hope were reliant on human efforts, it would be fragile. We are imperfect beings. We falter, break promises, and lack strength. If hope rested solely on our shoulders, it wouldn't stand. But this indestructible hope is a gift from an unwavering God. You can embrace this hope in its entirety—it's inward, outward, and upward. You can experience it daily, abundantly, and eternally. So, why would anyone settle for less? Don't let your aspirations be limited. If your perspective of God is constrained, it's time to dream bigger and welcome His boundless hope. Life is fleeting. Heaven awaits. Let this new habit be your gateway to God's indestructible hope.

Cultivating Hope:

1. What is an indestructible hope?

2. How can one encounter with Jesus or a Bible verse change you?

3. How can you begin to share your story with more people?

Bible Study Questions:

1. What are all of the roles of a good shepherd?

"'I am the good shepherd; I know my sheep and my sheep know me—just as the Father knows me and I know the Father—and I lay down my life for the sheep. I have other sheep that are not of this sheep pen. I must bring them also. They too will listen to my voice, and there shall be one flock and one shepherd." (John 10:14-16)

2. How is Jesus the ultimate source of hope?

"Do nothing out of selfish ambition or vain conceit. Rather, in humility value others above yourselves, not looking to your own interests but each of you to the interests of the others. In your relationships with one another, have the same mindset as Christ Jesus: Who, being in very nature God, did not consider equality with God something to be used to his own advantage; rather, he made himself nothing by taking the very nature of a servant, being made in human likeness. And being found in appearance as a man, he humbled himself by becoming obedient to death— even death on a cross! Therefore God exalted him to the highest place and gave him the name that is above every name, that at the name of Jesus every knee should bow, in heaven and on earth and under the earth, and every tongue acknowledge that Jesus Christ is Lord, to the glory of God the Father." (Philippians 2:3-11)

3. What do you learn about the hope of God from His name?

"For to us a child is born, to us a son is given, and the government will be on his shoulders. And he will be called Wonderful Counselor, Mighty God, Everlasting Father, Prince of Peace." (Isaiah 9:6)

4. How are the promises and hope of Jesus connected?

"'Do not let your hearts be troubled. You believe in God; believe also in me. My Father's house has many rooms; if that were not so, would I have told you that I am going there to prepare a place for you? And if I go and prepare a place for you, I will come back and take you to be with me that you also may be where I am. You know the way to the place where I am going.'

Thomas said to him, 'Lord, we don't know where you are going, so how can we know the way?'

Jesus answered, 'I am the way and the truth and the life. No one comes to the Father except through me.'" (John 14:1-6)

5. How can you spread hope and glorify God?

"Then Jesus came to them and said, 'All authority in heaven and on earth has been given to me. Therefore go and make disciples of all nations, baptizing them in the name of the Father and of the Son and of the Holy Spirit, and teaching them to obey everything I have commanded you. And surely I am with you always, to the very end of the age.'" (Matthew 28:18-20)

Scan this QR Code to dive deeper with Jesse and watch his video that provides additional stories, insights, and a prayer:

CONCLUSION

Thank you so much for investing the time and energy in engaging your heart and mind as we walk down the road of hope together. Jesus is The Way. Abiding brings hope. You are loved, and your story is significant. God blesses you to be a blessing to other people. Your story is connected to how God will bring hope to your friends, relatives, acquaintances, neighbors, and co-workers. When you love your neighbor and share your journey, they will be inspired, and hope will multiply. Hope is available. Hope is relational. Hope is habitual. Hope is indestructible. Hope is contagious. Hope changes the culture. Hope brings out the best in other people. Hope encourages and empowers. Hope is transformative in the deepest ways. Hope heals. Hope unites us. Hope is like jumping into a refreshing lake of God's goodness, grace, promises, and presence. My prayer is that you have clarity and take the next steps as you desire hope, discover hope, and develop hope.

I encourage you to put your trust in Jesus and walk closely with Him. There's no greater love. There's no greater gift. There's no greater sacrifice. There's no greater provision. There's no greater peace. There's no greater relationship. There's no greater grace. There's no greater demonstration of hope. That's what you find in Jesus. Hope overflows from the inside out. Don't compartmentalize your relationship with God into one day, one hour, or one place. Abide with Jesus where you live, work, learn, or play. Enjoy a 24/7 relationship with God. The truth is, on our own, we run dry. We run out of patience. We run out of love. We run out of hope. Our lack of hope reveals our need for God. We can't share what we don't have. When you put your trust in Jesus, the Holy Spirit dwells in you. God is one in three persons: Father, Son, and Holy Spirit. You do not have to do this alone. You do not have to live alone. The Holy Spirit is going to comfort and empower you.

There was a point in my life where I felt hopeless because I had lost so much. What I learned is that some things can't be taken away. I will always be loved. God is with me. My life always has a purpose. I can always have a good attitude. I can always pray. I can always worship. I can always have great relationships. I can always serve. I can always listen. I can always forgive. I can always live with passion. I can always choose generosity. The most important things in life are solid and protected. Because of that, we have hope. God is the anchor for our souls and brings a secure identity and a lasting hope. God has made all of us to receive and give hope every day.

Next Steps

As we conclude, I'd like to leave you with some practical tools to cultivate as habits in your life. I challenge you to incorporate these into your daily routines as you continue on a path of indestructible hope.

1. **Inward Hope: Start utilizing *The Power of the Second Thought* in your daily life**. God has already planned incredible victories for you and placed them in your path.

"For we are God's handiwork, created in Christ Jesus to do good works, which God prepared in advance for us to do." (Ephesians 2:10)

Hope is all-encompassing: it celebrates the past, makes the most of your opportunities today, and walks with confidence in God into the future. Joshua faced a challenging new season as his mentor Moses passed. This was the season for Joshua to step up in inspiring ways. God wanted to lead the people into a new space with new blessings. A generation wandered in the wilderness, not trusting God for the promised land.

But Joshua and Caleb were different. For Joshua, the key was the renewal of his mind. God told him to meditate on His Word. Every time fear, worry, despair, excuses, distraction, and doubts entered his mind, he could think about scripture and God's promises. *The Power of the Second Thought* would help Joshua flourish. But beyond the miraculous events, the daily practice of intentionally choosing God's Word was crucial. As you think, so you live. Hope begets hope, leading to growth, success, and transformation.

If the vast potential of hope feels overwhelming, remember to be faithful to the tools God has given you. Your new habit is practical and achievable. When you excel in small things incrementally, the implications are monumental and profound. You'll consistently do what many only do occasionally. Start with one intentional second thought. Repeat this habit daily. Soon, you'll recognize and identify destructive thoughts, reject them, and replace them with thoughts that align with heaven, bringing hope, truth, and life. This habit leads to restoration and an overflow of hope.

For additional encouragement, check out my TEDx talk on Hope Habits, which you can find by scanning the QR code at the end of this chapter. This message will further reinforce the topics and insights we have covered in the book together.

Join me on my weekly podcast, TheBonfire.org, where we gather, grow, and experience more of God's presence. My passion is to provide content that will ignite hope and a fire in your soul. You have been given a roadmap, a new habit, resources, and most of all, God is with you. Now, it's your turn to move forward and live what you have learned.

2. **Outward Hope: Intentionally give hope to others every day.** If you have gained hope, share this book and the resources with friends and family. Consider guiding someone through the book. This collaboration will strengthen your bond. Hope starts with receiving, and then God brings an overflow as you give hope. You can start by having discussions about hope in

your home and practicing hospitality. Hope travels through relationship risks and rich conversations. Hope invites and provides. Expand your vision of hope globally. Be faithful and trust God with the results. He can do more than you can imagine.

When you walk with God, and your mind is renewed, there are no limits to what God can do in and through you. You'll feel more alive as you experience more of God's hope. You were made to live a life of hope, to encourage and empower others, and to bring out the best in them. Intentionally look for opportunities to generously bless people. Take the initiative, and see how God moves in your life.

3. **Upward Hope: Start with the most important aspect of your life, your relationship with God**. You can choose to follow Jesus if you have never made that decision. Know that He died for your sins and overcame death and the grave. This is a covenant relationship, and no one else can force or make this decision for you. Is anything preventing you from saying, "Yes" to Jesus? You can put your trust in Him as your Savior and Lord right now. I would be honored if you let me know if you have just made that decision. When you begin a relationship with Jesus, you have peace with God and the forgiveness of all your sins. You are in God's family forever and will spend eternity in His presence. If you have been walking with God for years, but are not growing in your faith, it's time to develop new habits and a deeper relationship with God during the week. You can abide with Jesus in all places and create a spiritually healthy environment at home.

A helpful resource that I created for you can be found by scanning the QR code at the end of this chapter. The video is titled, "How to be sure you will go to Heaven." It clearly covers the decision to follow Jesus, the assurance of salvation, and how to strengthen your relationship with God. I have designed additional free resources to help you walk daily with God, including an eBook I have written to develop this most important relationship in your life. Many people have come alongside me to strengthen my faith, and I will never forget that. It's my honor to be there for you and provide practical tools. I encourage you to find a healthy and solid local church, too, where you can connect and serve. You can find all of the free content and video series on my website, including how parents can train and encourage their kids to follow God: jessebradley.org. You can also contact me on social media @jessejbradley. I truly care about you and want you to have all the hope God offers. God is the source of this hope, and your primary role during the day is to abide with Him. God's greatest gift to us is His presence.

Filled with Hope

I want to pray with you as we move forward with new hope:

"Gracious God, thank you for my brothers and sisters who are desiring more hope, deep in their souls and in their daily lives. My prayer is that we will enjoy abiding with You, Jesus, and will experience an abundance of hope. We don't have all the answers or know how every detail of our stories will unfold. We are seeking You with our decisions and asking for wisdom. We will not worry about tomorrow but remain present in the moment with You and are grateful for today. We ask for Your help with cultivating new habits and experiencing growth and vitality. With the new victories You bring, the powerful transformation, and the fire in our souls, we will give You all the glory. As hope is developed and amplified, we want to bless people locally and globally. We know there are no limits to what You can do in and through us. We commit to a life of generosity. We don't want to be passive and harbor negative first thoughts. Instead, we will intentionally replace them with second thoughts that align with heaven, full of love and truth. Thank You, God, for the foundation and the fountain You bring as You are writing a script that is full of hope. We will share our stories, humbly serving with the strength and courage You give us. Thank you, God, for indestructible hope. We know the end of the story couldn't be better; each day is an amazing opportunity, and the best is yet to come. We pray this in Your name, Jesus, amen."

Cultivating Hope:

1. What is your plan to develop your new habit of *The Power of the Second Thought*?

2. Who do you want to invite to journey with you and hold you accountable for the next steps?

3. What have you learned about hope, and how are you inspired by the hope that God provides?

Bible Study Questions:

1. What are some benefits of deciding to follow Jesus?

"Very truly I tell you, whoever hears my word and believes him who sent me has eternal life and will not be judged but has crossed over from death to life." (John 5:24)

2. Who will help you grow in hope and hold you accountable?

"As iron sharpens iron, so one person sharpens another." (Proverbs 27:17)

3. What has God made clear for your next steps forward?

"If anyone, then, knows the good they ought to do and doesn't do it, it is sin for them." (James 4:17)

4. How will you live as an ambassador of Jesus, the hope of God?

"Therefore, if anyone is in Christ, the new creation has come: The old has gone, the new is here! All this is from God, who reconciled us to himself through Christ and gave us the ministry of reconciliation: that God was reconciling the world to himself in Christ, not counting people's sins against them. And he has committed to us the message of reconciliation. We are therefore Christ's ambassadors, as though God were making his appeal through us. We implore you on Christ's behalf: Be reconciled to God. God made him who had no sin to be sin for us, so that in him we might become the righteousness of God." (2 Corinthians 5:17-21)

5. How is God encouraging you both through The Power of the Second Thought? How is He encouraging you to make a difference in this world?

"Be strong and courageous, because you will lead these people to inherit the land I swore to their ancestors to give them. Be strong and very courageous. Be careful to obey all the law my servant Moses gave you; do not turn from it to the right or to the left, that you may be successful wherever you go. Keep this Book of the Law always on your lips; meditate on it day and night, so that you may be careful to do everything written in it. Then, you will be prosperous and successful. Have I not commanded you? Be strong and courageous. Do not be afraid; do not be discouraged, for the Lord your God will be with you wherever you go." (Joshua 1:6-9)

Scan this QR Code to dive deeper with Jesse and watch his video that provides additional stories, insights, and a prayer:

APPENDIX - HOPE VERSES

A Menu of Options for Your Second Thought

God will uphold you:

"So do not fear, for I am with you; do not be dismayed, for I am your God. I will strengthen you and help you; I will uphold you with my righteous right hand." (Isaiah 41:10)

God helps you overcome fear:

"For God has not given us a spirit of fear, but of power, of love, and of a sound mind." (2 Timothy 1:7)

Jesus gives you peace:

"Peace I leave with you; my peace I give you. I do not give to you as the world gives. Do not let your hearts be troubled and do not be afraid." (John 14:27)

God is your refuge:

"God is our refuge and strength, an ever-present help in trouble." (Psalm 46:1)

God will guide you:

"Trust in the Lord with all your heart and lean not on your own understanding; in all your ways submit to him, and he will make your paths straight." (Proverbs 3:5-6)

God gives you a way out of temptation:

"No temptation has overtaken you except what is common to mankind. And God is faithful; he will not let you be tempted beyond what you can bear. But when you are tempted, he will also provide a way out so that you can endure it." (1 Corinthians 10:13)

God gives you wisdom:

"If any of you lacks wisdom, you should ask God, who gives generously to all without finding fault, and it will be given to you." (James 1:5)

God will display His goodness:

"I remain confident of this: I will see the goodness of the Lord in the land of the living. 14 Wait for the Lord; be strong and take heart and wait for the Lord." (Psalm 27:13-14)

God will renew you:

"Therefore we do not lose heart. Though outwardly we are wasting away, yet inwardly we are being renewed day by day. For our light and momentary troubles are achieving for us an eternal glory that far outweighs them all. So we fix our eyes not on what is seen, but on what is unseen, since what is seen is temporary, but what is unseen is eternal." (2 Corinthians 4:16-18)

God sings over you with joy:

"The Lord your God is with you, the Mighty Warrior who saves. He will take great delight in you; in his love he will no longer rebuke you, but will rejoice over you with singing." (Zephaniah 3:17)

God's love drives out fear:

"And so we know and rely on the love God has for us. God is love. Whoever lives in love lives in God, and God in them." (1 John 4:16)

God will reward you:

"Let us not become weary in doing good, for at the proper time we will reap a harvest if we do not give up." (Galatians 6:9)

God has good plans for you:

"'For I know the plans I have for you,' declares the Lord, 'plans to prosper you and not to harm you, plans to give you hope and a future.'" (Jeremiah 29:11)

You are God's masterpiece:
"For we are God's handiwork, created in Christ Jesus to do good works, which God prepared in advance for us to do." (Ephesians 2:10)

You are more than a conqueror:
"No, in all these things we are more than conquerors through him who loved us." (Romans 8:37)

God empowers you:
"Finally, be strong in the Lord and in his mighty power." (Ephesians 6:10)

God has called you:
"But you are a chosen people, a royal priesthood, a holy nation, God's special possession, that you may declare the praises of him who called you out of darkness into his wonderful light." (1 Peter 2:9)

God shelters you:
"Whoever dwells in the shelter of the Most High will rest in the shadow of the Almighty." (Psalm 91:1)

God comforts you:
"Praise be to the God and Father of our Lord Jesus Christ, the Father of compassion and the God of all comfort, who comforts us in all our troubles, so that we can comfort those in any trouble with the comfort we ourselves receive from God." (2 Corinthians 1:3-4)

God is kind with you:
"Because your love is better than life, my lips will glorify you." (Psalm 63:3)

God provides for you:
"And my God will meet all your needs according to the riches of his glory in Christ Jesus." (Philippians 4:19)

Jesus always loves you:

"For I am convinced that neither death nor life, neither angels nor demons, neither the present nor the future, nor any powers, neither height nor depth, nor anything else in all creation, will be able to separate us from the love of God that is in Christ Jesus our Lord." (Romans 8:38-39)

God will renew your strength:

"Do you not know? Have you not heard? The Lord is the everlasting God, the Creator of the ends of the earth. He will not grow tired or weary, and his understanding no one can fathom. He gives strength to the weary and increases the power of the weak." (Isaiah 40:28-29)

You are a new creation:

"Therefore, if anyone is in Christ, the new creation has come: The old has gone, the new is here!" (2 Corinthians 5:17)

God has compassion for you:

"Cast all your anxiety on him because he cares for you." (1 Peter 5:7)

Jesus gives you rest:

"Come to me, all you who are weary and burdened, and I will give you rest. Take my yoke upon you and learn from me, for I am gentle and humble in heart, and you will find rest for your souls. For my yoke is easy and my burden is light." (Matthew 11:28-30)

You are secure in God:

"I give them eternal life, and they shall never perish; no one will snatch them out of my hand." (John 10:28)

God lifts you up:

"But you, Lord, are a shield around me, my glory, the One who lifts my head high." (Psalm 3:3)

You are God's ambassador:

"We are therefore Christ's ambassadors, as though God were making his appeal through us. We implore you on Christ's behalf: Be reconciled to God." (2 Corinthians 5:20)

You are talented:

"Each of you should use whatever gift you have received to serve others, as faithful stewards of God's grace in its various forms." (1 Peter 4:10)

God saves you:

"For it is by grace you have been saved, through faith—and this is not from yourselves, it is the gift of God—not by works, so that no one can boast." (Ephesians 2:8-9)

God gives you hope:

"May the God of hope fill you with all joy and peace as you trust in him, so that you may overflow with hope by the power of the Holy Spirit." (Romans 15:13)

God establishes you in His love:

"For this reason I kneel before the Father, from whom every family in heaven and on earth derives its name. I pray that out of his glorious riches he may strengthen you with power through his Spirit in your inner being, so that Christ may dwell in your hearts through faith. And I pray that you, being rooted and established in love, may have power, together with all the Lord's holy people, to grasp how wide and long and high and deep is the love of Christ, and to know this love that surpasses knowledge—that you may be filled to the measure of all the fullness of God. Now to him who is able to do immeasurably more than all we ask or imagine, according to his power that is at work within us, to him be glory in the church and in Christ Jesus throughout all generations, for ever and ever! Amen." (Ephesians 3:14-21)

God fills your heart with love:

"And hope does not put us to shame, because God's love has been poured out into our hearts through the Holy Spirit, who has been given to us." (Romans 5:5)

Jesus gives you peace:

"Peace I leave with you; my peace I give you. I do not give to you as the world gives. Do not let your hearts be troubled and do not be afraid." (John 14:27)

Jesus gives you abundant life:

"The thief comes only to steal and kill and destroy; I have come that they may have life, and have it to the full." (John 10:10)

God hears your prayers:

"Therefore I tell you, whatever you ask for in prayer, believe that you have received it, and it will be yours." (Mark 11:24)

God is your source of joy:

"Until now you have not asked for anything in my name. Ask and you will receive, and your joy will be complete." (John 16:24)

God opens doors for you:

"Ask and it will be given to you; seek and you will find; knock and the door will be opened to you." (Matthew 7:7)

God satisfies your soul:

"Blessed are those who hunger and thirst for righteousness, for they will be filled." (Matthew 5:6)

God gives you eternal life:

"But whoever drinks the water I give them will never thirst. Indeed, the water I give them will become in them a spring of water welling up to eternal life." (John 4:14)

God gives you His presence:

"If you then, though you are evil, know how to give good gifts to your children, how much more will your Father in heaven give the Holy Spirit to those who ask him!" (Luke 11:13)

Jesus gives you living water:

"On the last and greatest day of the festival, Jesus stood and said in a loud voice, 'Let anyone who is thirsty come to me and drink. Whoever believes in me, as Scripture has said, rivers of living water will flow from within them.'" (John 7:37-38)

Scan the QR Code Here:

I am grateful you have read this book! My prayer is that you are filled with hope that is indestructible both daily and eternally.

As a thank you, please scan this QR code to access free resources on hope! This includes my "7 Days of Transformation" video series and content related to personal development, inspiration, faith, family, and relationships.

If The Power of the Second Thought has been valuable to you, please consider sharing it with your family and friends. I would appreciate it if you could leave a kind review on Amazon.com with your feedback. It will help us bring hope to more people!

Made in United States
Troutdale, OR
10/28/2023

14084907R00100